Conversations
on Writing Fiction

Conversations on Writing Fiction

*Interviews with
Thirteen Distinguished Teachers
of Fiction Writing in America*

Alexander Neubauer

 HarperPerennial
A Division of HarperCollinsPublishers

HarperCollins books may be purchased for educational, business, or sales promotional use. For information, please write to: Special Markets Department, HarperCollins Publishers, Inc., 10 East 53rd Street, New York, NY 10022.

FIRST EDITION

Designed by Alma Hochhauser Orenstein

Library of Congress Cataloging-in-Publication Data
Neubauer, Alexander.
   Conversations on writing fiction : interviews with thirteen distinguished teachers of fiction writing in America / Alexander Neubauer. —   1st ed.
     p. cm.
     Includes bibliographical references (p.) and index.
     ISBN 0-06-273223-4
     1. English language—Rhetoric—Study and teaching—United States. 2. Fiction—Authorship—Study and teaching—United States. 3. Creative writing—Study and teaching—United States. 4. Authors, American—20th century—Interviews. 5. English teachers—United States—Interviews. I. Title.
PE1405.U6N48 1994
808.3'007'073—dc20   93-25533

94 95 96 97 98 ❖/CW 10 9 8 7 6 5 4 3 2

For April

The ideal condition
Would be, I admit, that men should be right by instinct;
But since we are all likely to go astray,
The reasonable thing is to learn from those who can teach.

—SOPHOCLES, *ANTIGONE*

A creative-writing class may be one of the last places you
can go where your life still matters.

—RICHARD HUGO, *TRIGGERING TOWN*

CONTENTS

ACKNOWLEDGMENTS

My continued thanks to the thirteen writers in this book who gave so generously of their time and wisdom and opened the doors to their classrooms.

Also, more than I can tell them, to family and friends—writers all (if not always writers)—Carla Stevens Bigelow, Edward Bigelow, Brooke Stevens, Joshua Neubauer, Sheila McCullough, Peter Post, Allen Kurzweil, Cyndi Stivers, John House, Nancy Bleemer, Gino Diiorio, and Tamara Weiss. My deep gratitude to Pamela Bernstein, Nell Goddin, D. W. Fenza, and Michael Morse, who helped so much in the budding stages of this project; to Mel Berger at William Morris; to Robert Wilson, my editor at HarperCollins, for his good thoughts and encouragement, and to Ralph Martin for the same.

Special thanks to the many writing students in various settings for sharing their insight into classes, teachers, and the process of learning itself, among them: Karen Anway, Peter Brown, Tim Carroll, Susan Chamandy, Lauri Feldman, Erika Gentry, Julia Johnson, Kristen Kammerer, Todd Kiman, Peter Lefkowicz, Lauren MacIntyre, Michael Norman, Adam Ross, Tiffany Thraves, Anita Thompson, Assaf Urieli, and Alec Wardwell.

Finally, most of all, to my wife, April Stevens. She knows why. And to my father, Peter Neubauer, who believes in everything that has never been said before.

INTRODUCTION

This is a book about thirteen writers who are also thirteen teachers. It is about skill and wisdom, craft and art, and about how those qualities are learned and passed on to creative writers in this country.

We have an old, lingering image of writers. Unlike dancers or musicians, with their ballet masters and maestros alongside them, writers are thought to learn their craft alone—on fire with passion or ideas, suffering if possible, isolated from the rest of the world. They might be apprenticed at a newspaper (as Hemingway was) or work days in an insurance office (Kafka), but the notion of writers receiving formal guidance in a classroom seems to contradict our own lasting image of them; it contradicts imagination itself. "Writing cannot," the feeling goes, "just be taught."

The thirteen writers in this book offer different but definite responses to that feeling. Collectively, through self-reflection sometimes vivid, theory sometimes grand, and the reality of the classroom never far from view, they convey not only the fact of teaching but also the many and various approaches to it. "Can writing be taught?" people still ask. Simply put, some of the best American writers have now learned to write their fiction "in school" and gone on to teach in one. The writing class is, in many ways, an American phenomenon.

Perhaps it began in the late 1930s at the University of Iowa, with Norman Foerster and Paul Engle usually getting much of the credit. By the late 1960s about one dozen writing programs existed in this country. Today over three hundred colleges and universities offer official programs, many for graduates hoping to pursue creative writing as a vocation. Add to this total 82 colonies, conferences, and centers for writing, as well as uncounted informal, independent workshops, and one gets a sense of this largely new, decidedly American cottage industry.

"Can writing be taught?"

The question today, for both interested readers and writers—especially writers looking for a setting in which to study that fits their particular needs—is rather "How?" How are students with differing degrees of ability and passion helped to layer those qualities onto the page? How does any one human being impart to another the uses of imagination, dedication, patience, or linguistic flair? And how does a teacher find the right measure in his or her approach to one individual, helping him hone a craft, practice an art?

Violinist Itzhak Perlman once distinguished between two of his music teachers, one a man, one a woman, by saying: "She asked, he told." That essential difference is only one among many. While some teachers use the traditional writing workshop, others experiment. While some emphasize technical and editorial skills, others are also concerned with a student's character; some are improvisational in class, others methodological; some forceful, others intentionally passive—and on and on.

More than anything else, what I hope readers will find here is a variety of original views about the art and craft of writing—and original voices to go with them. For as one listens to good teachers, and as one begins sitting in on recommended classes, their methods often seem no more important than the teachers themselves—their experiences and personalities, their flexibility and dedication. George Garrett, who is represented here, has written that success in teaching depends more on "the man himself than the system he works by or with." A few pages of reading in this book may prove him right. Regardless of shared theory or intent, one is left finally and happily with thirteen disparate, singular views. From quiet to cunning to wise, it is their voices you will hear.

Who are these thirteen writers and teachers?

As practitioners of a difficult art, that of *writing* fiction, they are probably well known to you. As past or present practitioners of a second, perhaps equally difficult art, that of *teaching* others to write, they may strangely be unfamiliar. Yet in their dual roles they are able to describe a process they have lived and today witness: the creative writer in his or her becoming.

T. Coraghessan Boyle, a one-time student of John Irving's, started a powerful undergraduate writing program at the University of Southern California in 1978, which he still heads. Stanley Elkin, a vibrant teacher, a one-time student of Randall Jarrell's, has been "pointing out the beauties" in his students' stories at Washington University for years. Gordon Lish's famous and rigorous independent classes are as different from Jane Smiley's—based on her own original, uncritical method at Iowa State University—as hers are from Nicholas Delbanco's, whose long view of the writer's life, generous and knowing, is again particular to his own history. George Garrett's improvisational, play-by-ear teaching style influenced R.H.W. Dillard, director of the jewel-like Hollins College program, and Dillard and Garrett both influenced Madison Smartt Bell, who at Hopkins, Goucher, and elsewhere offers an informed view all his own. John Irving and Gail Godwin, classmates at Iowa and students of Kurt Vonnegut's, no longer teach writing formally but remain full of insight into the learning process and the writing class itself, its possibilities and limits. Clarence Major, at the University of California at Davis, and Rosellen Brown, at the University of Houston, writers of both poetry *and* fiction, speak

eloquently and individually about the nature of creativity and
the meaning of a writing "career" for those setting out on one.
And Eve Shelnutt, breaking new ground at Ohio University,
here offers a fully realized, inventive alternative to the American
writing workshop.

Needless to say, there are many good, highly regarded
teachers across the country, and I have not tried (except a bit
geographically) to represent them all or the schools where they
teach. What follows is one list only (arranged alphabetically), a
taste of a taste of what goes on in American classrooms. Originally limiting myself to a dozen writers, ending with a baker's
dozen, I have made some obvious mistakes of omission. For
instance, I have chosen teachers who are primarily fiction writers (short stories and novels), leaving out with distress those
good teachers known mainly for poetry, such as Tess Gallagher,
William Stafford, and Pearl London. Other names surely
belong, and some are honored here as the teachers of these
teachers: Stephen Koch of Madison Smartt Bell, Robert Pack of
Rosellen Brown, Fred Chappell of Eve Shelnutt, John Updike of
Nicholas Delbanco. Others are at least mentioned, including
Toni Morrison, Marie Ponsot, Russell Banks, Amy Hempel,
Robert Coover, David Huddle, Ron Hansen, Frank Conroy, John
Casey, and the late Wallace Stegner, whose prized little book *On
the Teaching of Creative Writing* was useful to me in this project.

In an effort to be fair, I've also left out The New School, my
own home base in New York City, which has a wonderful array
of accomplished teachers.

The point again is this: Good teachers abound, both close to
home and across the country. For writers seriously looking for a
school, a teacher, a structure, or some clues to get started, perhaps these conversations will prove helpful in that way. Every
student must ultimately find someone with whom the fit is comfortable, selecting, as John Gardner said, "his writing program
on the basis of its teachers, hunting out those whose interests

seem closest to his own." Teachers are people and people are finally themselves. Like looking for a good psychotherapist or heart surgeon, it pays to shop around. Since most of us know little about the many official programs nationwide, not to mention the independent ones, I have also included some minimal factual information about current writing programs at the bottom of most of the biographical introductions. The best and most useful guide, however, is *The AWP Official Guide to Writing Programs,* which contains descriptions of all the hundreds of creative writing programs in the United States and Canada. (Its address may be found in the Selected Bibliography of this book.)

Still, that old image of writers not needing teachers lingers both here and abroad, no matter what one says. Any college or country that presumes to teach writing opens itself to a controversy. "Don't (American) programs and workshops mainly produce 'assembly-line' stories, or 'minimalist' stories, or 'merely competent' stories?" people still ask, underscoring Flannery O'Connor's thought from 1961:

We want competence, but competence itself is deadly. What is needed is the vision to go with it, and you do not get this from a writing class.

Critic John W. Aldridge's most recent book is called *Talents and Technicians: Literary Chic and the New Assembly-Line Fiction* (1992). Others have echoed his fear that American writing programs may produce "mediocre writing-school fiction." A recent PEN/American panel discussion was titled "Are American Writing Programs Good for American Writing?"

Anyone interested in reading contemporary American fiction, certainly anyone interested in learning to write it, may weigh these questions with care. I have tried, somewhat neutrally, to draw opinions about them. Still, my own bias—from my experience writing fiction as well as visiting many of the classes across the country offered by these teachers—is that, in so many ways, a writing class simply works. It provides structure where often there is none; it offers solace and camaraderie; it demands production. And if the teacher is also a good writer— as these teachers are—he or she may provide the bonus of serving as a model for all to emulate, a "shine on the apple," as T. Coraghessan Boyle mentions here. Perhaps it is true that artistry cannot be produced in a year or two of workshops. Perhaps it cannot be *produced* at all, anywhere. Yet good teachers, the kind you will meet in these pages, provide enormous guidance, and I come away feeling its abiding value.

Mostly after the tape recorder was turned off, Gordon Lish made the point that the experience of his classes was different each time, and that, like all true experience, it was finally outside his description. He has a point. The test of any active teacher, represented in these pages or not, is finally day to day, with students getting the chance to become better writers, or seers, or readers, or people—in whatever combination, to whatever degree—every time they go to class.

This book is merely an expression in words of thirteen living examples of an ongoing process, namely teaching writing, just as the act of learning to write fiction is itself a living process *and for anyone who wants to try,* which may be the best thing to remember.

Madison Smartt Bell

Madison Smartt Bell was born in Williamson County, Tennessee, in 1957. He received his B.A. summa cum laude from Princeton University and his M.A. from Hollins College, which is where he began his first published novel, *The Washington Square Ensemble* (1983).

As one of the most productive young writers in this country, Bell so far has written seven novels (including *Soldier's Joy*, which won the 1989 Lillian Smith award, and most recently *Save Me, Joe Louis*, 1993), two collections of short fiction (*Zero db*, 1987, and *Barking Man*, 1990) and two screenplays. In "Less Is Less: The Dwindling American Short Story" (Harper's, 1986) he examined the limits of "minimalist" fiction, and in these pages he underscores his enduring belief in "the total pie of literary possibilities" for American writers.

Madison Smartt Bell has been an active teacher of creative writing since the Stonecoast Writers' Conference in Maine, where he learned "how to do tutorials [by] watching George Garrett work." Along with his wife, the poet Elizabeth Spires, he is presently writer-in-residence and Director of the Creative Writing Program at Goucher College. He is also visiting associate professor at the Writing Seminars in Johns Hopkins University and has taught, among other places, at the Iowa Writers' Workshop and the Bennington Writing Workshops at Bennington College.

This conversation followed one of his Bennington workshops.

Goucher College, in Towson, Maryland, offers a B.A. in English with a concentration in Creative Writing (poetry or fiction). Johns Hopkins University, in Baltimore, Maryland (The Writing Seminars), offers a one-year M.A. in fiction, poetry, nonfiction prose, or science writing.

Q: You've spoken highly of George Garrett, who was one of your early writing teachers. I'd be curious to know where you were in your life that made such a writing class fruitful.

Well, I was a sophomore at Princeton and I hadn't written very much fiction at all. I was good at doing expository writing, the kind of thing that you learn to do at school, and I came to Princeton wanting to write fiction—only to discover that you had to apply separately to get into the writing program. I didn't realize that and was so intimidated that I left for a semester and wrote a bunch of short stories and came back and was duly admitted to George Garrett's class.

He was a very easygoing teacher in the sense that he didn't put pressure on people to write in any particular way. His whole theory was to see what a person was naturally inclined to do and try to help them refine whatever their talent or ability led them to produce, and that's certainly the tack he took with me, usually very gently. He exerted a huge influence on my behavior as a writer.

Q: You've said that his students write like themselves and not like him.

Yes, this is the thing. There are a lot of students of his out there and many of them teach writing. I'm really of the third generation, I think, of people who have been influenced by him. In the first wave there were people from U.Va. [University of Virginia] and Hollins. People like Richard [R.H.W.] Dillard, who now runs the Hollins program, and Henry Taylor, Kelly Cherry from U.Va., Alexander Theroux, and a great many other people. And their teaching style in general—this is particularly true of Richard and I think also of Henry—is simply a *laissez-faire* approach, to see what students are going to do and try to help them refine their technique. It requires a lot of self-motivation on the part of the student. You can't really come in blank and expect that you're going to get help. You're certainly not going to get any cure for writer's block unless you ask for it. You basically have to come up with your own thing; you have to have that much energy.

After there's a text in hand, George or Richard or I will help you read it and understand it and then you see perhaps how you can make it better. But the effect of this, too, is that unlike a very directive teacher who will say prescriptively, "do this and don't do that," it's difficult to trace the writers [who come out of this method] through their work. You can trace them pretty easily through their teaching style. I was also Richard Dillard's student, as I say, and that had a great effect on me too and affected the way I teach. But as far as the work goes, you can have all different kinds of writers. Richard, for instance, writes as differently from George as you could possibly imagine; I write very differently from him.

So it's not the kind of easily traceable, identifiable, stylistic descent that you would find in the followers of Gordon Lish, for instance, where there's a fairly strict editorial policy operating. He attracts a certain kind of student and, having attracted that kind of student, forms them in a certain way. There are many teachers out there who are like that; Lish is just an extreme example, from what I know. There are others where it's not quite so concentrated or high profile. And for many people there's nothing wrong with that. But it's nice for people to know what they're in for if they go to a teacher like that, because there you do get molded.

Q: In a more "open" style of teaching, though, can you convey a message or leave an imprint on a student who needs it? How do you know when to stand back and when to jump in?

Well, it's improvisational, requiring cooperation and intelligence on the part of the group, their willingness to be truthful without being cruel. It also helps if the teacher isn't particularly sadistic, I think. And you saw how it went today. What I tend to try to do is get the people in the group to interpret the story in some way and see if they can do it. Where they have problems doing it is likely where there are problems in the story, if there *are* any problems.

So I like to think of the <u>teleology</u> of the whole story pretty early in the group discussion, which is ultimately not what a lot of teachers do. A lot of people start with a cloud of detail and try to build up to a general vision. I'm usually more comfortable going the opposite way.

Q: And what if you get a group of less motivated students?

Sometimes undergraduate workshops *are* more inert, so I tell more stories myself, maybe, and there's more whip cracking. I have some drills, not drills for actually writing their own things but writing exercises to do on each other's work to make them think about it harder.

Q: Your philosophy of teaching was influenced by George Garrett, but isn't it also a matter of fitting your personality?

I guess it is. I was looking at him, and everybody else I studied with as a writer either was somebody who he'd influenced or had a similar attitude naturally.

The other person who affected me a lot as a teacher was Stephen Koch, who's director of the Columbia [University] writing program, and he was at Princeton my senior year. He did something which I admire and which I also try to do, which was to look at my work—one hundred and eighty degrees away from his own, completely different—and really understand it on its own terms and see what it was trying to do and help me with it. At that point I was very incoherent about my own contentions. He was looking at some badly organized stuff and he really did help me get a clearer sense of it. One of those kindly, optimistic teachers who proceeds on the assumption that the story can work, as opposed to the kind of teacher who presents you with some adversity to overcome.

Q: Going back to what you were saying about looking at the teleology of the story first, I noticed in the workshop today that in each one of the stories presented you got your students to identify the kind of story being discussed, whether it was a "bait-and-switch story," "a romance," "a learning story."

My feeling is that they were able to do that on their own without me totally cramming it down their throats, although I did try to achieve my own interpretation, too. And in the last story, my understanding of it changed as a result of the discussion because there were a couple of people who had noticed things that I had not.

As I say, if you get a good group it's like jazz improv and you all end up somehow playing the same tune but preserving some kind of individual quality at the same time. And maybe that's something not all teachers do. Many teachers only understand and are interested in a limited section of the total pie of literary possibilities. Not that they are all only interested in the very thing they do—you know, if it isn't pretty much like Raymond Carver, we don't like it—but maybe they go only about ninety degrees either way from that, [leaving] a whole half of the situation they really can't deal with. Indeed, there are certain things I am not very expert in, like surrealism or Pynchon-esque, Coover-esque metafiction; that kind of stuff is hard for me. I mean, I try to deal with it. It's not that I don't like it, but it's not where I'm most comfortable, so it's hard for me to follow the student down that path.

Q: Today you were directive, you played an active role with the class, but you rarely used qualitative words for a story, like "good" or "bad."

Of course there are a lot of students who believe that they want to be told either a "yes" or a "no." I will probably tell students "yes," but I'm reluctant to tell them "no," especially in a general way, because a lot of people who I indeed thought were hopeless basket cases surprised me by forging themselves into very presentable, publishable writers over the period of a few years. Never underestimate *desire*. Often more important than talent, it turns out, oddly.

But the other thing about today's situation was that the second pair of stories really were finished. It's hard to get workshops to recognize finished work and accept it as such because they are designed to be fault-finding machines and they will function that way whether there are faults or not.

. That is, in workshops you are rewarded for success and punished for failure, and one of the things this leads people to do is stop attempting what they don't initially do well. Which is very limiting. So you have to try to fight that somehow, but it's difficult because it's hard to change the fundamental nature of a group that tends toward *consensus*. And that's the stated goal, consensus, you want that. But aesthetically, consensus is not necessarily good for the individual writer. So now I always tell people, usually at the beginning of the assembly of the group, "You must understand that ninety percent of what you hear will probably not be relevant or useful. And you have to be able yourself, as a student, to discriminate the useful advice from the useless advice."

Q: Including . . . ?

Including mine. Now of course in practice I don't behave as though I believe that. I try to present my own case, my own reading, as persuasively as I can. But I started thinking about the importance of discriminating between good and bad advice when I was teaching at Iowa, when I saw that there were so many talented students there and yet so much writer's block. Say what you will about Iowa, they do get the best students in the country because almost everybody wants to go there. Despite the size—around fifty students in fiction in a two-year program—everybody has written at least one publishable piece of work, otherwise they wouldn't have gotten in. Nevertheless, when I was there a lot of people were doing just dandy but some others were screwing up. I knew as a kind of statistical fact that out of the twenty-five people who graduate from there every year, most of them are not going to publish a first book. I mean, they just won't get that far. And I thought, "Hey, why is this, when I know that everyone was capable of it when they arrived?"

And it's not just Iowa. I don't mean to say that it is; it's sort of generalized through the whole business of the national workshop system or whatever you want to call it. But I do think that the answer to that question has a lot to do with stubbornness— that the people who do survive and go on to publish are people who resist the group, resist advice, don't pay any attention to anything unless it really strikes to the core and they have an authentic inner response: "Yes, you're right." That's not going to happen every time. What's more likely to happen is a mood of kind of depressed confusion, where students say, "It didn't work out as well as it should have, they didn't really get it, one person says the story should move north, the other says south, what should I do, try to please them both?" The people who survive don't listen to that.

And I didn't either, you see. I was in rather less workshops as a student than probably most writers my age who came through the educational program at all. But in the ones I was in, I tended to discount a lot of what I was told—even at Hollins, where I loved and respected almost all the people in the group, as well as Richard. You know, they'd say all this stuff and I'd just smile and go write another fifty pages. I'd never change anything. Later on I did ... some things. [Laughs.]

Q: In your opinion, then, is the workshop method the best way of going about teaching writing?

Well, the problem is that just because of numbers and time and what kind of work people can be paid to do, workshops are the only way that's really possible. Certain things are good about them. It's nice to feel that you are in a group of like-minded people, up to a point. But this is the thing John Aldridge is complaining about; he thinks you should feel indeed like you're an alien and a misfit because you're a writer, that this is a really weird thing and no one else does it. And I think he does have a point there. The way in which workshops do provide support systems for the ego perhaps takes too much of the edge off the business of training yourself, which is what you have to do whether you're in a workshop or not. That's what it comes down to.

But I also think it is psychologically helpful to people, and strengthening, to feel that they're not freaks, that there are other people who do this, that someone will listen, even in a kind of artificial environment, and that they can try out the effect of their work on a reasonably intelligent audience who will talk back to them and tell them how much they've understood.

Q: But if a large part of it has to do with simple personal stubbornness, is it really necessary to seek out a place like the Iowa Writers' Workshop—or might any place be as good as any other?

I think Iowa is a very good place for somebody who wants to be in a large pond. I would not have enjoyed being a student at Iowa because of the way I'm constituted. I know some people who really like it. I liked Hollins, a small unpressured program where there are about fourteen students, everybody was very friendly, it was not at all competitive, there wasn't an agent or a publisher's rep. within a thousand miles. Iowa is a very visible place and there are certain kinds of pressures there. Just being surrounded by dozens of writers who are as good or better than you can be intimidating for some people. I don't think I would have enjoyed that; it might really have spooked me and given me problems. I liked being the best on the block. I'm an egomaniac, in my own sweet and nice way. [Laughs.]

But a lot of people really thrive on it and it makes them work harder and more. So you have to figure out which one you are before you decide if you want to go to Iowa or another program.

Q: And clearly you can get something of the group experience you speak of just about anywhere.

Yes, both good and bad, that's certainly true. Whereas being a *teacher* at Iowa, I love. I mean, you get to work with great students; they're all good.

Q: Since you've commented on it in print, let me ask you about Eve Shelnutt's criticism of the workshop method as the best way of going about bringing writers along. She incorporates outside reading to a much greater extent and eliminates class criticism of students' creative work.

Yeah, there *is* another way, and I'd like to try it someday. I think William Gifford is still running a very successful class somewhat like that at Vassar and I've heard of other people who've done it, too, mostly people who would now be in their sixties or no longer teaching. You'd have a reading list of works which perhaps in some way were indicative of technique, and people would simply show their work to the teacher—and there would be private meetings and that would be it. Or variously you'd have half a class of literature and you'd workshop some at the end. I've actually taught a class that was like that at Hopkins, that started off with a reading list and ended with a workshop, and I'm interested in going more in that direction. It might be a way to take some of the problems out of the workshop method.

I liked Eve's article a lot ["Notes from a Cell: Creative Writing Programs in Isolation," in *Creative Writing in America*, 1989]. I thought she made some good points and at the end observed a real problem, but I think she stated an incorrect solution. She seemed to think that the answer was for writers to get more involved with theoretical criticism. That's wrong.

But she did put her finger on this really nasty problem, which is that to the same extent people in English departments have become more and more hermetic, incomprehensible and disinterested in looking at the literature of their own time. The writers in writing programs have become more intent on talking only about the making of their texts and reading each other's work in workshop situations. So there's this ghastly hole in between these two situations. That writing and reading are considered to be two different activities, a straight divorce, is ridiculous. Reading literature for the pleasure of being instructed, to paraphrase Horace, is something that's just not being done in education anymore.

I did have one student at Goucher who hadn't ever been in any creative writing classes, but the first story of his that I ever saw was brilliant, a great story. And what he had done was *read* what he liked and try to learn from and build himself around it. The people who'd really influenced him were Flannery O'Connor and Gogol. An interesting combo and not all that unlikely if you think about it. I thought, "Hey, this guy has done something for himself that's not happening in the typical workshop environment."

Eve's right, it's terrible and damaging when you have a complete schism between reading and creative writing. But I'd like to think that this hegemony of critical theory is a temporary phenomenon. It's been finished in France for quite some time and surely it can't go on forever here.

Q: On that note, what about the hegemony of writing styles and fashions? What about the influence on young writers of trends in writing such as . . . you know what I'm going to ask, don't you?

It's just that I wrote a single article ["Less Is Less: The Dwindling American Short Story"] in 1986!

Q: And you're forever getting prodded about it. But just to the extent that so-called minimalism has been linked to American writing workshops and sometimes labeled as "assembly-line fiction," is it a problem? Or is it permissible for young writers to pass through a stage like that?

The infamous essay didn't really criticize minimalism, which I think has its place. You have to realize that what you're really dealing with there is reified Hemingway. [Raymond] Carver was the person in that whole group who really understood what was happening; he was very conscious and deliberate about that and took some Hemingway tactics and changed them and adapted them very deliberately for his own purposes. I don't think Amy Hempel necessarily realizes that she's writing Hemingway stories. She writes really brilliant Hemingway stories and she's good. But that's a very small segment of what you can do with a short story, and we're talking about short stories here.

What moved me into attack mode was the way it had eaten up the whole pie, obscured everything else, this kind of statement being made by the publishers that there were no short stories from about 1945 until [Jayne Anne Phillips's 1979] "Black Tickets" came out, disregarding Grace Paley, Peter Taylor, George Garrett, Andre Dubus, all these great writers who were just being ignored, some of whom continue to be ignored. That I thought was bad.

It turned out, though, that because of this wave of excessively homogeneous sort of work, all of a sudden short-story books became generally popular and a lot of more interesting writers like Mary Hood and Ellen Gilchrist and Louise Erdrich suddenly began to be recognized. I published my first book of stories in this climate. So in the end some good was done, and some greater variety was accomplished than how it looked at the time. At least people like Andre Dubus, who had not had any recognition, were suddenly recognized in this atmosphere.

By around 1990 you could look back on those years and say, "Hey, it's not after all such a bad thing."

Q: Were writing programs also responsible for the explosion of minimalist fiction, in addition to the publishing world?

Well, OK. A characteristic of the classic minimalist story is to concentrate exclusively on action and dialogue, action and dialogue. Of course it's not true of Carver; but for some of the younger writers who came up through the workshop mill, yeah, they were affected. The workshop rewards you for success and punishes you for failure. My experience with beginning students is that what they mostly do badly is summary exposition. Action and dialogue most of them can do, if not well, then better. So they are continually being shocked in the Skinner box of workshops for doing summary exposition, and when they do action and dialogue they get a food pellet. So therefore they very quickly just abandon any attempt to learn how to do summary well at all, and they write these very cinematic kind of stories where every transition is a jump cut—and you're simply witnessing these actions through a transparent window and frequently very tonelessly, with no voice shaping it much.

What happens then is very much like theater. Andrew Lytle, another person who has influenced me quite a bit, pointed out that what fiction really *is* is summary. This other stuff, action and dialogue, *that* comes from theater, that's where we get it. So a novel has these theatrical elements combined with the ability to write summary exposition. If you look at the short story in particular, I don't think anybody knows how to write summary anymore who's under sixty. Elizabeth Spencer writes beautiful stories that are controlled by voice and summarize long periods of time, and so does Peter Taylor. And people in England can do it, like William Trevor, because they don't have that workshop sense and I think that's part of it. But there aren't any young guys here who can do it; it's an atrophied skill, and I think that's sad.

Q: Since you mentioned a number of Southern writers, is there a regional or Southern gift for exposition and for summary, in a kind of Faulknerian way?

No, I don't think so. I don't think it's regionally typed. It's typed by time periods more and probably by the way in which movies were assimilated into fiction and the way it's cross-pollinated back. If you go and read any nineteenth-century novel, everything is summarized, there aren't any jump cuts, every transition is controlled for you by the writer, who frequently walks on stage and says, "Here I am, I'll tell you what's happening. . . ."

Q: And Hemingway cut that out.

Yeah, Hemingway cut all that out and gave us a very lean, mean, efficient story, which was good; but to regard that as an evolutionary step I think is sort of cracked. There are a lot of limits to it, and to say you can't go back and use the central-intelligence concept of Henry James is silly. I think you ought to be able to do that. That's what Peter Taylor can do—what very few others in the United States know how to handle. I'm not saying writers should go back and try to be like Anthony Trollope and stand inside the book and manipulate it, although in fact the most interesting writer in America right now is doing that, William T. Vollman. I don't know where he got his education. I guess he was educated as a scientist, but what he's doing with fiction is much more liberating than anything that's happened for a long time.

Q: And what happens in your classes if you get that Carver-esque story?

Hey, if I can get something at that level of accomplishment from a student, I'd jump for joy. Carver was a master at what he did. More often what you get is sort of bad imitations where you can't tell what's happening because nothing happens.

Q: Would you push a student away from even a good imitation?

Well, I don't know. I just hope they won't do it on their own. The way writers used to be educated before there was a workshop on every corner was to apprentice themselves to other writers whose work they liked. People do that with Carver and if they survive, it's going to be just a phase they go through. Carver is somebody who survived his influence from Hemingway. A. E. Hotchner is someone who didn't. There are dozens of guys like A. E. Hotchner who ran around writing Hemingway-like stuff in the forties and fifties when he was big. [But] the only reason I can remember A. E. Hotchner was because Paul Newman sued him over the salad dressing. So you don't really have to shoot those guys down, they're going to eliminate themselves. And along eventually will come somebody who will take the Carver thing and steal it completely and do what Carver did with Hemingway.

Q: Wallace Stegner said that the actual writing of the country "is incorrigibly closer to life than the fads are." It sounds as if he felt people weren't really following the fads anyway, at least in a meaningful way.

Well, I think he must have felt that it would be extremely temporary and the whole thing would be sort of self-correcting, and in a way I think that's how it's turned out. A lot of this doesn't have to do with the way writers work anyway but with how the publishing business works as a business, which is not very salubrious. It has a tendency to hype one thing over another at all times and they kind of switch around what it is that they're trying to promote, so usually the majority of good writing is getting the cold shoulder in that way, and it does go through these cycles. If you take the long view, which Stegner certainly would, then it's really, "Why worry?"

More serious I think is the kind of postmodern attitude that it is impossible to go back in literary history and build on the achievements of some earlier period. Which is really dumb, but it's a much more influential idea among writers, the Idea Used Up, what Charles Newman calls "can't-go-backness." [It's as] if you thought: I can't go back and build off of what Thackeray did in *Vanity Fair* because since then we've had Hemingway and since then we've had Barth and Coover and Pynchon.

But you *can* go back, because it's not teleological, it's cyclical, and people do fail to understand that and that's unfortunate.

Q: Isn't literary style evolutionary at all?

I don't think so. I mean, I accept that the novel isn't dead right now, that fiction isn't dead, but I do think if you look at the whole course of human history, it hasn't been around for all that long. I don't think it will be around forever.

Q: I'd be interested to hear how you fit your own writing into this, which is multistyled in many cases; there are times when it seems to have a Southern voice and others when it doesn't at all. Is any kind of regional voice something you encourage in a classroom?

Yeah, I guess I have a special affection for Southern voices and I guess for urban voices, too; but in my own situation as an apprentice writer, I was so excessively well informed about Southern writing, having read a whole lot and studied it academically and very thoroughly as an undergraduate, that it was very difficult for me initially to even think of writing anything in a Southern setting that wouldn't sound derivative. So my first really mature work grew out of New York City, a setting plenty had been written about but that I hadn't read. I was safe in that sense. As a third or fourth generation of Southern renaissance writers, it's hard not to see your turf diminishing, if that's the limit that you've put on it. After I'd written some books and had some confidence, I felt, "OK, I can go back and use my own country, my own people, I can write about that. I have the power to do it and do it my own way."

Q: Don't you feel the publishing world looks for local voices? For a while there were all those stories coming out of Maine.

The rebirth in regional writing was pretty salutary, really, and interesting. There is no reason for it to be parochially Southern, although Southerners have succeeded in making it extremely well known that the peculiarities of their region and the people in it are interesting to them and to other people, too. What they had in common with the great Jewish writers of the forties through the sixties was a kind of experience of disenfranchisement. America did not serve that up to the whole spectrum of the population until fairly recently. And so the effects on literature, I think, will be interesting. The voices that began to talk five or six years ago were very much coming from the invisible poor: Carolyn Chute, Elizabeth Moore....

Q: I've heard of your willingness to involve yourself with your students' work, even to the extent of helping some students get published.

Well you know, one of the reasons is that a lot of people did that for me. George did that for me, particularly. Stephen Koch certainly helped me pragmatically in very significant ways. So I *owe*. I think a lot of students get frigid treatment from their teachers in career matters and therefore are not motivated to behave any better themselves when they become teachers. There's no reason to be afraid of helping people or sharing information. The truth is I can't help people that much. All I do is introduce people to agents or give them the names of magazines. That doesn't cost me anything. And it's pleasant.

I'm certainly not the most saintly character.... But it would be nice if writers helped each other more, and indeed, people on the Garrett–Hollins axis tend to do that, so much so that at times it appears to be conspiratorial. But a lot of it is just friendliness. It's not a clique, it's not a cabal in the sense that we all have an aesthetic program that we're trying to promote, or some particular point of view. Why not help people who are good writers, whose work you like, if you can?

T. Coraghessan Boyle

T. Coraghessan Boyle was born in 1948 in Peekskill, New York. As a singer, rock drummer, and self-professed "complete degenerate and maniac" in his youth, he attended the State University of New York at Potsdam to major in music, graduating instead, in 1970, with a degree in English with Creative Writing. Two years later he was accepted by the Iowa Writers' Workshop, where, as a student of John Irving's and others, he received his doctorate in nineteenth-century English literature. Immediately afterward he was hired to start an undergraduate creative writing program at the University of Southern California in Los Angeles, and he continues there as a teacher of intermediate and advanced workshops.

Beginning with *Decent of Man* (1979), a collection of stories written mostly during his years at Iowa, Boyle's work has received a growing national and international readership and critical success. He is the author of the story collections *Greasy Lake* (1985) and *If the River Was Whiskey* (1989), as well as the novels *Water Music* (1982), *World's End* (which won the PEN/Faulkner Award for Best American Fiction in 1988), and *East Is East* (1990), among others. His most recent work is the novel *The Road to Wellville* (1993).

Boyle speaks here of the possibilities of classroom learning ("We're creating, I think, a new generation of writers who are very sophisticated") and of the traits necessary for both good writing and good teaching. This conversation took place in Los Angeles after an advanced undergraduate workshop of high caliber and palpable enthusiasm.

The University of Southern California offers a B.A. in English with an emphasis in Creative Writing. A Master's of Professional Writing (M.P.W.) is also available from the graduate school.

Q: John Irving, a teacher of yours at Iowa, said, "Tom Boyle surely didn't learn much from me." He meant, I think, that good writers can only be encouraged a bit, a technical problem or two highlighted. That's what Kurt Vonnegut seemed to have done for him.

And that's exactly what John Irving, John Cheever, and Vance Bourjaily did for me at Iowa. Exactly. I agree with that; however, I think I do *a lot* for my students. I don't know if they learn from me except by example. You know, here I am, I did it, they can do it, too. But, see, they're undergraduates and I see them develop. I nurture them. Some of the people you saw in that room today have been with me three consecutive semesters—once in their intermediate and twice in the advanced class, which is as long as they can go.

Q: That's almost as long as a graduate program.

Exactly, and if they do four original stories each semester and study with me four times, they've got a book done—as *undergrads*. I think what I *can* do for them, particularly because they're undergraduates, is help them to develop. They might develop without my help if you just put them in a closet and said, "Look, every time you put a story out this slot we'll give you food and a hundred dollars." [Laughs.] But I think I can help them accelerate the process of making those little discoveries. Sitting there as a student and mulling over the problems of someone else's story doesn't necessarily translate into fixing your own story, but at least you're involved with the process and you can think about it. We're talking about an art that comes from the unconscious, after all.

Q: Irving, of course, must also have served as role model. That has an effect, too.

When John Irving was my teacher, he was the guy who had been at the workshop and published two novels, which in itself was incredibly impressive. John was working on *Garp*. In fact he used to read sections to us. He's a sincere artist who does what he wants, got the public attention, and has been very, very generous to people who haven't got the public attention. And that's part of being a teacher, too. Maybe he didn't like teaching, but as far as being an example and mentor, he's A-plus. Of course, you don't have to be a famous writer to teach, but for well-known undergraduate writer teachers—Joyce Carol Oates, Russell Banks—I think it's an extra shine on the apple. The students envision what they will be like someday; *they* will sell the books.

Q: Teaching and writing is a good combination for you, then.

One of the reasons that I enjoy it here is that I am as engaged intellectually as my students. You can see the way the class went, even though it was the first day: All but two people spoke. That's great participation. I'm not prodding them; they just get involved intellectually and that's great. See, a lot of writers' personalities do not accord with that sort of thing and that's why they became writers in the first place. That's fine. I'm half and half. I'm sort of a showman, I love to perform, I love to go on stage, and I love an audience. I could never give this up, no matter what. I could see giving just one class instead of two, but I love it. It's exciting.

And I'm a little different in another way, too. I got my Ph.D. in British literature of the nineteenth century. I thought of being a teacher from the very beginning, and when I began here my writing income and teaching income were exactly equal. It was a profession and a career. Now it's more of a hobby. In fact the hardest thing for me—the reason why I will cut back to one class at some point—has been the huge acceleration of publicity since about '87 when *World's End* came out. This fall, for instance, I had to cancel two weeks of classes to go to Germany on a book tour. Those classes I rigorously make up, because I feel if they pay the money to see me, I will be in that room.

Q: Stanley Elkin said he couldn't get the momentum going to start a novel during the months he was teaching. He could do stories but not a novel.

[Bernard] Malamud said the same thing, that he would not attempt to write while teaching. I fortunately have gotten used to a certain level of production during the semester and feel very comfortable with it. From the beginning I've done it hand in hand; I know no other way. So I'm not like Malamud or Elkin in that respect. I feel fortunate I can do both.

Q: Let me ask you more about your style of teaching. The laid-back, noninterventionist, "Kurt Vonnegut" approach that John Irving and Gail Godwin enjoyed at Iowa might not work as well for undergraduates, who, as you say, may need more nurturing. On the other hand, your students seemed highly capable. How active do you have to be?

Today, for instance, they talked for a long time about the first of the four stories and I didn't have to say much. As it wears on, however, I have to say a little bit more and prod them more. The best classes work when I say the least; and the author of the story knows how I feel about it because I write him a thing *this long* and correct every error. I think it's just a question of force of personality, of experience—developing it by trial and error over time—and enthusiasm. Maintaining enthusiasm is important, too.

Q: And picking good students, obviously.

Well, maybe we're lucky because we've established the undergraduate program and there's a huge number coming up. When I began the program in '78, I was teaching the whole thing; now there are stiff requirements in order to advance.

Q: Your students today used a vocabulary of analysis with confidence: "theme, lexicon, form, character, patterns." Especially in the first story.

It was also the best story, I think, and the most successful, so they analyzed it in an appreciative way. Let me tell you what I thought of the four stories today real quickly. It'll help.

The first story I thought was the best. In fact the student blows me away. This guy is one of the best I've ever had; he's great. He's experimenting. He's never done a story like this before, in three voices. There's a very tight weave of the message of the story throughout, the characters totally realized. You take that and mail it to the magazine. It's golden.

The second writer again has an amazingly subtle ability to work with image and symbol and make the story resonate with it. What was missing—and she's subtle and I've missed some of her work before by judging it too quickly—was the moment of epiphany. But that story is about two beats from being fully realized.

The third story wasn't yet close to being what it should be. I read four student responses out loud, and three of the four said they needed to hear more specifics. The story has to be totally reworked.

And then the last story. . . .

Q: That last story, which people seemed to like the least, got a lot of attention, too.

Because they trust the author, they've seen his work before. I admire and like him; he is using the workshop in the most intelligent way. And it's this: He could put a story up for workshop and people would fall over dead and say, "This is terrific." And he has. But he's beyond that. His ego is not engaged at this point. He wants to experiment, and he's experimenting with the sort of thing he did today. I think he's gone way overboard, and he and I talked for a long time after class and he explained to me what all the symbolism meant. And I pointed out to him that twenty people read the story twice and wanted to appreciate what he was saying, but none of us got it. *None.* So he's got to reevaluate. That's as far as the workshop can take you. And I think that's valuable for him.

Q: In class, though, you didn't comment directly to the author. No one did. Is that a rule?

I used to be more democratic. Now I refuse to hear the author talk. It's not relevant. The author's words have to communicate to the audience *on the page*; that's what this is all about. The author uses *us* as his guinea pigs. We could ask the author, "What did you mean here?" and clear up the whole problem and stop the discussion, but that's not relevant. What's relevant is for the author to discover what intelligent people think he or she meant, then they can go from there.

I also prepare them professionally. I go through every line, and it's got to be perfect. I'm very hard on them in that sense. There's none of this "we love you, Joe, and we love your story." That's useless to everybody, and I've been in workshops like that, everyone so supportive, loving each other. Great. But what's accomplished? Nothing. I'm very tough line-to-line. This is professional. On the last day of class I give them a speech about publishing: how you go about it, how I went about it, what the chances are, the competition, and so on. The second story today. She's a superb writer, but I was shocked at the mechanical errors in the story. Maybe it's the first week and she rushed to put it up. But I don't tolerate that.

Q: You mean more than spelling. You mean . . . ?

Yes, felicity of phrasing—that's all got to be taken care of. Otherwise, I would like to be noninterventionist in class and basically elicit their responses. The author knows how I feel, and in some cases the author and I have worked on the story together. He or she has come in and said, "Look, I'm stuck, I've got two pages, what am I going to do?" and I'll say you might do X, Y, or Z. They don't have to follow that advice, but maybe it stimulates them.

But in class I don't want to propound the system. There *is* no system. Everyone has his own individuality and his own perspective on what's going to happen. I think, if I'm a good teacher, I have a very catholic approach. I think some of the most brilliant writers often don't make good teachers because they feel so strongly about their own aesthetic that they can't view other types of work as being worthwhile. So they make clones and groupies of themselves. I've always been very afraid of that. I'd like to think—maybe I'm deceiving myself—that I can keep my predilections and prejudices in check and have a given writer develop excellence in his or her own way without making them clones of the type of writing that I do.

And there's another thing to speak to. There is a rap in America *and* in Europe (but a deep curiosity, too, particularly in Germany and Japan, where people are fascinated): "What is this phenomenon? How can there be creative writing in the university?" Obviously, there *is* creative writing in the university. We have a Shakespeare expert, a Chaucer expert—let's have a writer, too. I think that's good. They're fascinated to know how it can be part of the academy. It *can* be, on the terms that you saw today.

This criticism that writing classes only produce stories that please students. . . . In my estimation of my classes, that is complete and utter horseshit. The stories here are totally various and develop in their own way. There *is* no "workshop" story. These four stories you saw today are typical of what we will see: all different sort of things. Sure, they all take a Joyce course, they all write like Joyce for a couple of weeks. But I think that's great.

Q: Trends, fashions—do they enter in?

I'm not really affected by trends. If a student comes into my class and has read a lot of writers—Mary Robison, say—and writes in that style and it's great, hell with it, I'll praise them in everything they can do. That's fine. If there *is* a tendency towards a kind of workshop story, then it is the teacher's fault—

and we're talking about the sort of teacher who is a monumental figure, and maybe very brilliant, but only sees *this much* of the aesthetic window, and the student must be within that or they can't advance.

Q: And your style as a writer—your linguistic energy—my guess would have been that at least one out of the four stories, say, would have been . . .

Exactly like mine?

Q: Or trying to be. Nicholas Delbanco, in fact, said as much, that some students these days wanted to write Tom Boyle stories.

I understand that. Yes, I'm read and imitated. I'm very flattered, that's terrific. Maybe it will also inspire: "If this schmuck can do it, I can do it." You always think of your elders: "Yeah, this guy has accomplished this, but, hey, I'm only nineteen and I'm going to blow him out of the water." But I would be *disappointed* if they imitated me. I really would. Truthfully, I do get a couple of writers every semester who write in my vein, but I don't necessarily think they're imitating me: there's Kingsley Amis, Evelyn Waugh, García Márquez, there are all sorts of models that interest them. So I don't have a lot of students who come in here slavishly doing what I do. I really have a mix, as you saw today.

Q: Let me go back to what you were just saying about the criticism of the so-called workshop story. John Aldridge has been one of those critics, knocking quite a few well-known contemporary American writers who have come out of writing programs. You emerged unscathed. You do realize that you're one of only about two writers who got passing marks from him! What do you think?

Obviously, I think he's a great critic! [Laughs.]

He has a point in his book, actually, that a lot of what goes on from the publishers is hype. I'm very impressed, or I used to be, when I see in the front page of the review section a picture of a writer who has a new book out. I think, "That would be great." But in fact it's the publisher putting so much money into this or that person. Aldridge has a point. Where is the critical faculty? Where is it, who is it? You can't make a living as a critic. Harold Bloom? OK, there's a couple. Where's the critical apparatus, who's going to judge?

But maybe it will come from this legion of new, very sophisticated and great students. Still, at a certain level, no matter what you do, how sophisticated you are, how many classes you've taken, how many degrees you have, how brilliant you are, it comes down finally to, "Do you have this great talent or do you not?" I can't judge that. The world will judge that. At this level, I would never make that judgment.

I've also been stunned by students who barely made it and then a year later ... on top, the best. One guy in particular wanted this so intensely, had a lot of texture and great promise, but he wasn't there yet. He didn't make the grade into the class. He was a tough man, but he broke down in tears. I tried to console him. Next semester, however, he did make the grade, just barely, and by the end of that semester he was within two or three of the very best in that class. By the end of the *next* semester he's one of the best I've *ever* had. In one year's time. This is not something I did. I think the atmosphere of being there helped him to bloom at that moment. I would never presume to say, "Look, man, you don't have it," because I would be wrong, and I'm not God.

Q: So it was very much the program that allowed him the chance to do it?

Exactly. Almost every writer in my generation went to a writing program, or taught in one. The academy has sort of preserved us as a viable subject. I mean, people aren't really buying Chaucer today either, but he's preserved, thank God, for our culture. Writing in this generation has moved into the academic arena, and that's good. I would hate to think that literature is going to go the way of opera: If we don't buy our tickets and support the opera it's not going to exist anymore.

Maybe there *are* problems, too. Maybe we do have some mediocre teachers who have published one book of crappy stories that were just like the crappy stories in their workshop, and so now they're teaching a workshop to produce more crappy stories. However, maybe there's one student in there who is great and will revolutionize everything.

Q: So, with undergraduates especially, you keep yourself open to whatever they want to try?

I think I'm open to many different types of writing, and we each have our strengths and weaknesses. Perhaps one student has a tremendous strength for structure over language. I'm not going to say, "You, you're out of here." However, the ones who I *really* feel don't have it I will not encourage. But that's as far as I go in making that judgment, because they're young yet. In five years, who knows? In ten years, who knows? Like Allan Gurganus. Allan we didn't hear from for ten years. Then he writes his book. Again, who's going to judge? "Hey, Allan, you don't have it and you're not going to do it." It was *fifteen* years later, for God's sake.

Q: Well, how do you explain someone like Allan Gurganus, say, who was with you and Jane Smiley at Iowa but took years longer to emerge?

How do you explain someone like that? You wouldn't be an artist if you didn't feel somewhere in your heart that you're better than everybody else and you're going to blow them away and you are going to do it. Throughout my career, as a professor and as a writer, people said, "You idiot, how are you going to sell books—nobody knows how to read? And how are you going to be a professor—there are no jobs as professors?" I thought, "Yes, perhaps, but if one person is going to do it, it's going to be me." How do you explain it? There's great talent, and you can see it in a workshop like Iowa in my time. Great talent. Some develops. It's takes a fanaticism and a dedication and a single-mindedness.

Q: So you try not to judge, even when you could judge?

I'm one voice. Sure, I'm the professor, the famous writer, I'm giving the grades and running the course. But on the other hand, when it gets flowing, this person over there has a comment as valid as any I have. They're reacting as intelligent readers. That's what I like to get going. I don't want to control the class so much as I want them to express what they feel about strengths, weaknesses, this point, that point. Respect your teachers, as I did John Cheever, John Irving, Vance Bourjaily, but you have to have a chip on your shoulder, too. If a classmate says to you, "I think it should go this way in your story," then consider it. If, as in the case of the last student, twenty people didn't get it, he'll probably consider it real hard. But it's *his* story, ultimately, and nobody can tell him what to do with it, including me. I'm one of twenty.

Q: Did you yourself listen to anyone in school?

As an undergraduate at Potsdam College, in New York State, I barely made it though. I was a complete degenerate and maniac. I went to be a music major, switched to history, and then to English with creative writing. I was a very poor student and I think things were fairly rudimentary in those days, too. I never even saw creative writing until I was a junior in college. And I think this was reflected in the workshop at Iowa in my time. We had tremendous talent but not a lot of direction. What I got was what we said earlier: people whom I respected saying, "You're on the right track, go ahead." My students today are very sophisticated. Many of them have probably been taking creative writing from elementary school, for Christ's sakes. They're prepared to really think about and express what they feel. When I was a student, I would read my colleagues' stories and wouldn't know what to make of them. I mean, they just baffled me. I didn't know how to articulate what I meant. I rarely had anything to say anyway, didn't participate, and was uptight about it. These are my enemies, my competitors, I thought. I really didn't have a good attitude. You go to Iowa and every small genius from every small college is suddenly thrust together—and they're all geniuses, and who's going to be the genius who gets in the *Atlantic Monthly* first? Who gets the contract?

Q: What you said about the writing colony in East Is East: *". . . Brains fevered by dreams of grandeur, conquest, and the utter annihilation of their enemies."*

[Laughs.] Well, I don't have to deal with that with these undergrads, and that's refreshing, too. Here's another *amazing* thing. Often, like last semester, the class will go out afterward, when they get to know each other, and have a beer or something. I used to go with them on occasion, but I just don't have time. I regret it. They will go out as a unit and have a beer and hash it over; they will form splinter groups, meet on weekends. It gives them an identity and a community, you know.

Q: So what did you finally come away with from Iowa? It's considered one of the best in the country.

It is *the* best, by far and away. If it slipped a little bit during the tenure of the last director, right now with Frank Conroy I will tell you it is far and away the best. Nothing comes close. I was there in 1988 for his first semester and, as I said earlier, I never had a better class. Incredibly various stories, from surreal to hard-core realism and everything in between. They were great, brilliant. Frank Conroy feels very deeply about what he does, and about writing. He is as conversant with a full range of workshops and what goes into them as anybody I know and just as dedicated and interested and connected to his students.

So my experience at Iowa? My experience was, it saved my life. And I've done a lot of publicity for them and donated time—not my money yet, I'm not rich enough!—but it turned my whole life around. You know my history. I was shooting heroin, I was crazy, a degenerate. I hadn't taken GREs. Only applied to one graduate school—had only *heard* of one school. My heroes had been there: John Gardner, Coover. I sent them the stories and they accepted me. I will forever be grateful. Iowa gave me exactly what I wanted on my own terms.

And in terms of the quality of the students in my day—and I was there of course for five and a half years—there was Jane Smiley, Jayne Anne Phillips, Ron Hansen. Allan Gurganus. The people of our generation who are well-known writers, many of them were there.

Q: Did your own style emerge at Iowa?

It emerged in between undergraduate school and Iowa, when I went through this period as hippie, shooting dope and whatnot. I still wrote stories occasionally and still thought of myself as an intellectual, but I was hanging out with people where all we did was get as high as we could and listen to big music pounding through stereos. Still, somehow, I had this impulse to write. *Descent of Man* comes from that period. The stories that I sent to Iowa for admission, one of them is the last story in that volume, called "Drowning," which Cheever loved, by the way.

Q: I'm curious. What was Cheever like as a teacher?

Cheever was there our second year, fall of '73. Very drunk, very crazy, on the run. I, as a punk, didn't value him. I'd read his books; he was passé. I was into Coover and Barth and Barthelme and so on. But when he came out with the collected stories in '79 I was humbled, and I've taught him ever since. He is so great. You know what? When he and I would have a discussion and I would use the term "experimental," he would always get a little smile on his face and say, "Well, you know, *I'm* experimental." I'd say, "Horseshit." But in fact you read a story like "The Death of Justina" or "The World of Apples" and it just knocks you dead. He creates a new form in "The Death of Justina."

On the other hand, *I've* become less experimental over the years, because perhaps in my early career I was going to form and structure too much at the expense of character. I think there's a unity of modes and aspects that makes a great work of art, and hopefully you grow towards it.

Q: Your class discussed four of its own stories today. What about outside reading in a writing class? Who else besides Cheever do you teach?

At all levels I always teach literature in conjunction with the course. They read Kazuo Ishiguro's *Remains of the Day* last week, which is one of the best novels of the last decade. Maybe *the* best. I would rate it with Louise Erdrich's *Love Medicine*. A stunning work. And you should have read their essays about it. They loved the book. Only one person out of twenty didn't dig it. Then, as I get to know them, I point them to given books. And we always try to use literary takes. You know, "This reminds me of...." When it reminds them of TV I might be a little sarcastic.

But I teach what I read in the last year that blew me away. Usually in this class it's novels. In the intermediate class it's short stories. I select them for various styles—from the experimental, the comic, black humor, minimalists to realists. I've never taught a course in my life in which I didn't use a book by Raymond Carver, who, in my estimation, was the greatest story writer in our time, as John Cheever was in his time. I still teach Richard Ford, who may not be a minimalist exactly but is coming out of Hemingway, who invented it for our time. Hemingway is probably the most radical stylist in history, more so even than Joyce, coming out of the nineteenth-century novel. I like anything that is superb.

Q: And how aware are they, or how aware do you make them, of the commercial world in which they will have to write and compete?

At elementary school you let them be creative at the expense of form and technique. At this undergraduate level, I let them know that at the next level they're competing with the rest of the world to get into grad school, to publish. This manuscript that you give me must be perfect in every detail, as well as brilliant, as well as patterned, as well as flawless, every comma. When I give them the last lecture on publishing I let them know that the editor—and I was an editor at the *Iowa Review*—has a stack on his or her desk *this* thick. It has to be flawless.

Q: Punched up, too?

No, no. We're looking for unique art. That's what starts the movement, that's what sells, that's what's an expression of yourself. Not, "Oh shit, if I'm going to sell a novel I better write a thriller and calculate it this way." We're not interested in that. John Grisham is out there selling trillions of books. I don't care, my students don't care.

Q: A number of writers I've spoken with have mentioned writing as a career—a long view—where success can come in different ways at different ages.

Aldridge has a point here. There's a lot of hype involved. Publishers are selling books, here's this new guy, he's twenty-four, everybody's hyped, they're excited. They buy it. And of course I've gritted my teeth through each one of these manifestations of new writers. On the other hand, you don't want to be an athlete or rock-and-roll star, dead at thirty-two. It's a life's work. As in *East Is East*, writers will be jealous of one another in the colony. I tell my writers this, too. There's that to fight down.

It's easy to be generous and wise when you've made it. But getting there is tough. What it takes is the talent we talked about, which nobody can assess initially, and a complete single-minded perseverance. Many of the geniuses at Iowa never emerge. Writing wasn't a commitment. They did something else, became musicians or accountants. It has to be an obsession.

Q: So you go about writing your book and whatever happens to it happens?

If *The Road to Wellville* doesn't sell more copies than Stephen King, I'm killing myself. I'll be dead by the time this thing comes out! [Laughs.] No, actually, some of the greatest defeats I've had have turned out to be OK, turned out to be useful. You bear down and get tougher. I've made jokes about it many times. Sure, I want to sell more books than anybody, because you want to get the word out, you want to be the Messiah, worldwide.

In our parents' generation there was the idea of the proletarian writer. You didn't go to any fancy-ass college, you didn't discuss stuff. You went out and you lived, worked in the steel factory and wrote a novel. I don't think that happens anymore. Everybody goes to college and they get as smart as they can. I'm not saying writers are better now than ever. That's not true. There are always going to be some great ones and a lot that are mediocre. But at least there's a level of competence because we, as writing teachers, serve the purpose that editors did twenty, thirty years ago. What they're getting at the top level is of a certain quality.

And the positive side is—and I wouldn't be doing what I do if I didn't believe this—the cream will rise. We're creating, I think, a new generation of writers who are very sophisticated, and maybe one or two of them will do it. If you don't believe you can be a fat kid with a stepfather in Arkansas and go on to be president, then there ain't going to be any presidents. I think it's great!

A workshop may cheat people, but I don't feel like a charlatan because only ten percent will make their living as writers. I don't. I feel that I'm also helping society in this way—and helping writing—by creating an audience that has a deep appreciation of what's coming, a very sophisticated appreciation. I've had, I don't know, fifteen hundred, sixteen hundred students. Yeah, most of them are now sitting on the street with signs, "We'll work for food" or "We'll write for food." But I think it's a real, true audience that will spread and disseminate and help writing stay alive. Not just genre writing but real writing that has sophistication and intelligence.

Of course, you don't have to go to school to write. It just nurtures you and gestates—and how are you going to be earning your living in the meantime if you don't? One of the attractions of going to graduate school is that you have two years. You write a book and find out. And the academic world allows us that, too. I wasn't ready to go out and conquer the world with my stories in 1979. I published, but I didn't sell books. So the academic world has given legitimate writers a chance to have some time to work and develop. I'm pleased that my work is getting better and more attention instead of getting it all in one shot. You want that one shot. But you can't worry yourself about that. You just make art.

Every once in a while I run up against a journalist who doesn't get my act. Most do and that's OK, because I'm not really that modest. And then I get it back in print that I'm the most egotistical son of a bitch. You *have* to have a dedication and egotism that this is great work.

Rosellen Brown

(Photograph © 1992 by Keith Carter)

Rosellen Brown began writing poetry at age nine and stories (her first, a murder mystery) at ten, enjoying "the power of words deployed on the page for my own delight." At Barnard College she took an early and influential writing class, a poetry workshop with Robert Pack, and in 1962 received an M.A. in English from Brandeis University. She has lived since in Mississippi and New Hampshire, and currently teaches creative writing in Texas at the University of Houston.

Rosellen Brown is acclaimed for both her poetry, such as *Cora Fry* (1977), and her prose, including the novels *Tender Mercies* (1978), *Civil Wars* (1984), and most recently the critically lauded and best-selling *Before and After* (1992). *A Rosellen Brown Reader: Selected Poetry and Prose* (1992) reveals her twin affection, and she has been eloquent, here and elsewhere, in the need to traffic freely between forms whenever necessary. She has written, "If you, a fiction writer, are not prepared to make a set of poems out of your stalled novel, have you considered any of the other 'odd lots and broken sizes' of form that are so enticingly available to you?" Rosellen Brown's newest poems are a sequel to her *Cora Fry* and will appear next year in one volume together with the original work.

In these pages Rosellen Brown discusses the importance of flexibility in writing and also in writing programs themselves, where "all kinds of human purposes" may be served beyond more narrow, professional ones. In that sense, she offers a rare and wide view of the writing "career," both in its practice and its possibility.

The University of Houston, in Houston, Texas, offers a B.A. in English with a concentration in Creative Writing, an M.A. and M.F.A. in English and Creative Writing with a creative thesis, and a Ph.D. in English and Creative Writing with a creative dissertation.

Q: In your essay "Don't Just Sit There: Reading as Polymorphous Perverse Pleasure," you speak about the simple joy of one's early reading and writing and how to rekindle it in creativity. But I'm sitting with you an hour after you were on television with your novel, Before and After, *and I'm curious about the meeting of those two worlds, pure creativity and commercial success.*

Well, it's funny. If you could come up with the most seemingly classic, old-fashioned progression of a career it would be mine. I started as a poet, then started writing odd things that were neither poetry nor stories, then stories, and from there a novel and then more novels. It's almost a perfect curve. Except that it's not an inevitable progression or hierarchy, where one is better than the one before. I've just learned to go on longer and put together a larger scheme. There's value going back and forth, and after this book I'm going back to a book of poetry. I don't want to repeat even the possibility of another best-seller. People who write trying to craft their sentences carefully do it just because of the sound of the words, not because they've got their eye on the best-seller list. You have to keep that sense of self-delight. In some ways I still think of myself as a poet who writes prose, trying to revise word by word.

Q: You've written of "the astonished pleasure of the feel *of the letters," each letter even having its own color. But eventually writers have to narrow themselves.*

And we had to narrow ourselves too much.

Q: What do you see as the real gain of staying fluid?

The gain is that you can make use of more of what you are interested in. I think if you only write stories or only poetry, you let a lot of things go by, kinds of moments that might be usable for a poem, say, but not a piece of prose. If you keep all those options open to yourself, everything becomes usable grist. It seems a shame that so many people limit themselves. And I remember what it was like. I remember when I was in Mississippi in the sixties and found myself thinking what great stories there are here and what a shame that I only wrote poetry and didn't know how then to write stories.

Where I teach, at the University of Houston, we demand that our graduate students take what we call a crossover semester in another genre; the poets have to take a prose class, the prose writers a playwriting or a poetry semester, and so on. It's sometimes very difficult, but often they discover something they didn't realize they could do, just love it, and end up choosing to move formally from one genre to another. At the worst you won't write well in another genre, but you'll become more sensitive to what it takes for someone else to do it.

One of the things that's sort of a shame is that there's such a feeling of professionalism that it often isn't very inviting to experiment. Among teachers, too. The university hired a number of people who can easily do both, poetry and prose, but has always made it clear that we'd better stick to our own.

Q: Richard Dillard at the Hollins program told me that the teachers they hire have *to be able to do both, and that hopefully students learn from that.*

I once taught a course at Warren Wilson [College, a low-residency program in Swannanoa, North Carolina] that was on the edge between poetry and prose. How do you decide what form an experience demands? Make experiments, cross the line, straddle the line. One of the things that happens is that sometimes the most interesting fiction writers in my class are the poets, because they don't know much about conventional narrative writing. They're the ones who do experiment; they're much more tuned into words and interesting syntax and much less interested in linear presentation. They're the ones who feel around, leap the boundaries.

Q: Isn't that what the title of your essay was really advocating: "Don't Just Sit There"?

Yes. Steal from yourself, take chances, steal from others, put together collages made up of any number of things; but we get so locked in so terribly early, and when you look at the sort of standard story today, the quote–unquote *New Yorker* story—which we know does not really exist but is rather a shorthand for something else, today's Chekhovian story—what you find is that, good though many of them are, there's so little playfulness in them formally. They take a small emotion and may in fact make us feel it, but it's such a tiny little corner of what's possible. It's a shame.

Q: For those who want to experiment, I would think your career would make a good example.

But there are those who would say I'm not a great example because they don't think as much of my poetry as my prose, for example, and might say, "What's the sense of that, why doesn't she just do one thing and do it better, why do we need somebody who does something only half-well?" There are others who *like* my poetry. I get pleasure from doing both and not ever quite knowing what's going to come up next.

Q: I would think that the idea of playing fast and loose with genre, staying open to form, would have to be learned as a habit almost.

Well, I think you have to learn to think of yourself as a *writer* rather than either a poet or fiction writer. In the *Poets and Writers* directory they've got a "P" next to some names for "poet," but for the fiction writers they've got a "W," for "writer," not an "F" for "fiction." If you just think of yourself as writer you'll stay more loose and more open to whatever comes along.

Q: And now you are going back to writing poetry again.

Now I'm going back to poetry for a while, to a sequel to *Cora Fry*, which is a book of poetry I wrote after my first novel appeared. In *Cora Fry* one woman speaks all these poems, but there's also a story that gets told somewhere along the way; she talks about her life in a lot of little pieces, a mosaic, really, and then slowly a kind of story develops. The characterization was derived from my fiction, obviously, but these were poems. I wanted just then to get the voices of the novel out of my head, to get all that gray, covered-page feeling out, too. I conceived of it spatially before I had any idea what I wanted to do. I saw these tiny little poems on the page surrounded by white space. I was trying to be sensitive to what I needed sensually at that point, which was tremendous silence. And I was grateful that I knew something about how to write a poem, and also about how to do a narrative line. The best way to banish the static of a novel from your head is to leap back into poetry.

Q: Realizing that, commercially, you are sacrificing something?

Being on "Sonya Live" this morning or in *People* magazine last month is nothing I ever desired for myself—and still don't. It's something I have to get over. I don't consider it has affected my own response to my own work at all—and that's why I'm happy to go back into poetry. If it disappoints anybody, I don't care.

I think it was Toni Morrison who said, "I really don't have a *career*." And that's the way I feel. My agent can talk about what's best for my "career" if she wants to, but for me it's the metaphor of pulling words up from the well; if the bucket isn't empty, I feel very happy. It's always touch and go whether it's going to be there each time. There isn't any plan of what's good for a career because there *isn't* a career. It's just word after word.

Q: It's creating—?

It's creating. One of the things that bemuses me is when people talk of writing establishments—and they exist—having to do
with the politics of publication and of publicity and so on. But
the fact of the matter is, and maybe I take too generous a view
of writers, that I still tend to see them as much closer to the little girl in the essay you asked about: everybody still doing their
best to honor what they need to say. And it's never easy—unless
you're a hack writer who's got a formula. Everyone is worried
about whether what they write is something anyone would want
to see. And you worry just as much about the ninth book as you
do about the first. I'm starting number nine and I don't have any
guarantee that there's going to be something there. My last
book is in the desk drawer.

*Q: But you know whatever you chose to write now, based on the
success of* Before *and* After, *would get published and receive some
attention.*

But it could be horrible. It might not be a book that should
get published, and now there are all those people watching. You
still sit down in a quiet room with a blank piece of paper in front
of you and wonder if anything is going to materialize. One of the
things about writing programs that disturbs me a little bit—
among a lot of things—is that they make so very public your
desire to write, often at an early age, and you become answer-
able to all the bureaucratic necessities. I think it can do odd
things to the feeling that this should not be about making a
career, this is about writing what you want to write at a given
moment. There are times when my students are having trouble
producing what has to be produced for a given class. I want to
give them license to ignore it, but I'm often not able to do that;
they still have to come through; they'd better do their three stories, or whatever it is. And it's odd to me to have to place anyone
in harness and say, "You are now going to produce what they
ask I to." You really shouldn't answer to anybody but yourself.

Q: Do many of your students bring an uncertainty or fear, not only to create something good but also to sell it?

I think they do, sure. But I discourage people from thinking about it. We have, as does every writing program, a few students who are very concerned with and good at making connections, and I'm thus very disappointing to some people. But I don't ultimately feel that's the thing for them to do with their time just yet. It's very hard for me to remember when I was just starting out. Of course I must have wanted to publish the stuff—I sent it off—but I don't think I had more than the most modest ambitions for it; it didn't occur to me that there was a pot at the end of the rainbow. I never had a sense of deserving.

I mean, what was I? I was a kid from Queens who wanted to be a writer and so I wrote. I didn't have to sign up for courses, fulfill a requirement, or hang out with famous writers, which maybe was a shame because I didn't really have a role model. I had one teacher in college who was important to me, who made me learn to revise, and one other teacher for a shorter time, George P. Elliott, who taught me some larger things about the compassion with which you need to write, but it wasn't technical at all.

Q: Where was this?

This was at Barnard, and Bob Pack, who taught poetry, showed me how to sit still until I changed things fifteen times. I took the same poetry class with him three times, and that was it. I can't remember if I got into Iowa or didn't apply at the end, but one way or another I didn't go there, I went to Brandeis and was a Ph.D. dropout. There were a lot of people who wanted to write and dropped out of there one by one.

But undergraduate courses at that time were nothing like they are today, with undergraduate programs full of teaching stars. And if you go on to graduate school today you are sort of declaring yourself for a career. You want the handwriting to be on the wall and spell out your name. It was very different then. I knew nothing about marketing and so little about publishing, and there was nobody to guide me because I didn't know any writers.

Q: It wasn't an active decision you made, then, not to go into a writing program?

There wasn't much of a writing-program life at the time I was coming up. And then I lived in New Hampshire for many years. I did teach in the writing program at B.U. [Boston University] for a year, and in the first year of the Goddard MFA program. But I was only peripherally involved. I really didn't think of myself as a teacher. It was just: if you could, you wrote. And I'm still resistant; there are people at my program who laugh at me and think of me as the bad girl in a way, because I will tell students just as readily not to apply to graduate school. I'm not convinced it's a good thing for everybody. Some can use it and some don't need it.

Q: And then there's the question of finding the right teacher.

I think there are basically two kinds of teachers, and you've probably run into both kinds. There are the natural teachers, who teach out of their personalities and don't give a whole lot of thought to pedagogical method, they just *are*. Donald Barthelme, who taught at Houston, was like that. He would just stride into the classroom and bring himself along and not much self-consciousness about what he was doing; his opinions were very complex and useful and simply came out as they were. Someone like Gordon Lish is not to be confused with someone like Donald. Donald wasn't trying to impose a single method on his students. He wouldn't claim to know in the first sentence whether your story was worth writing or not. It was just that the force of his personality was so strong and the firepower of his opinions so uninhibited that [it] made him brilliant for some students and utterly useless for others. That is one way to teach, and it's for certain natural characters. You can't fake it.

And then there are teachers who take a more modest view, I suppose. I try most of the time to figure out what somebody's trying to do and help the person do that. And that means often that I may withhold my judgment of whether it's worth doing. In this I'm not that different from what my husband, who teaches high school English, sees as an ideal, which is not to impose too much from the outside but rather to lead people to understand what they're trying for and help them realize the means to achieve that end. That can sometimes be quite useful; it can also for some people be much less engaging and instructive than to have a master walk into the classroom.

In Donald's class, if he didn't consider students talented enough, they didn't get any of his attention. I've seen students come out of other classes just about vowing never to show anything again, and I don't think that's particularly productive. I tend to give everybody a good deal of attention, to get everybody to do the best that they can—I don't think I'm probably as effective with the ones who are incredibly smart and accomplished. But the fairly ordinary students will get more out of me because I have patience. I think of myself as a *teacher* in those situations.

Maybe in the end all you can say is that it takes many kinds of teachers. Students will find the ones they're most comfortable with.

Q: Is there an assumption in, say, a Donald Barthelme class that maybe the good students will go on to be truly good writers, and that the other ones. . . ?

Should probably be discouraged? And you *can* discourage them by ignoring them. Yes, I think that's the assumption. And I think it's a natural one for those kinds of teachers. My tendency is to feel that any student who is there is deserving . . . and it may be wrong! I'm not pulling for this as the only way of going about it. I'm also careful not to insult students and hope they go away.

Q: George Garrett said that writing programs shouldn't hurt *anyone.*

Right. Except for encouraging someone who maybe shouldn't be encouraged. But there too you want to say, "What's wrong with that?" "First, do no harm." I feel as if people's psyches could use nurturance. I've seen some students who I didn't think were promising turn a corner. I can think of two people in particular—I wouldn't have given a plugged nickel for their chances. But two people, after two years of graduate training, awakened one morning and said, "Oh, you mean you can make fiction out of *this*? Oh, well, in *that* case," and they went on to make wonderful stories. I don't know if it's the optimist in me. Maybe it's because my own work is often so horrible, and then it gets better when I sort of figure out what I'm doing; it makes me perpetually hopeful that someone who is really earnestly working very hard might figure out what needs to be done.

We're especially not hurting them in a place like ours, which is not expensive compared to a place like Columbia [University]. People do have to have jobs to support themselves here, but it's still not costing them ten thousand dollars a year in tuition. It's a state school. I think that's great. I know there are people who have felt very good about their capacity to work and finish a book—which may never get published but which will mean something in their lives. I don't mind having helped them midwife that to a kind of birth. Maybe you could argue that the world doesn't need any more of those mediocre books, but there are all kinds of human purposes to be served by this, and I cannot take the narrow view that I am only training geniuses. I've also seen very talented people fall by the wayside and less talented people continue and actually succeed.

Q: So then the question could be asked, why do certain critics and teachers and even some writing programs as a whole expect a kind of accomplishment at the age of twenty-two that other life professions. . . ?

Wouldn't *dare* dream of asking for! That's a very good question. And it's because people are not seeing writing within the context of the totality of somebody's life; they are trying to train winners. One of the things that just adds to that from the point of view of a faculty member is that university politics are such that you have to keep turning up dazzling success stories. There's one writing program that continually publishes an ad that says, "Our graduates have had twenty-three National Endowment grants, two Guggenheims, four this and thats." I think that is disgusting! B.U. started writing ads that I thought were rather more graceful; they said, "All we can promise you is a room with a view of the Charles," and "Some of the people who have taught with us are. . . " and "Some of the people who have graduated are. . . ." It's still immodest but less of an affront than giving you the bare numbers.

But the fact is that every time someone in our program wins or publishes something, we are obliged to put it in a newsletter, send a copy to the Dean, make sure that everybody notices—because we're always in need either of money or more faculty to run the program and you begin to traffic in successes. I understand politically why you have to do that, but from the point of view of that closeted hopeful artist alone with the words, that can make for a discouraging competitiveness.

And that's why—yes, you're right—we begin to ask for success at an age that's just preposterous. First of all, I wish we didn't even accept anybody to graduate school at twenty-two. I wish we said, go out and live a little bit and come back when you're thirty. But for all I know, what people are doing at this point will be useful fifteen years from now. I'm queasy, but it's one of the reasons I try to be as useful as I can to people who are not necessarily showing their stuff yet.

Q: I guess it also depends on what the stated goal of a writing program is, as to whether it answers its advertised purpose.

And I think if you quizzed us, you'd find differing answers.

Q: There was a PEN conference I went to entitled, "Are Writing Programs Good for American Writing?" And you can in fact question the question. Is their purpose to aid and abet American letters, or is it to help students somehow?

Exactly. Is it part of the life of a student to have a few years to write his or her best, hoping perhaps they'll like it and make it part of their future, or at least a constructive part of their present? Of course, you could say that graduate programs are all vocational in a sense. But writing is a tricky business. It's the engagement of a soul, and you can't rush your psychological development, your experience.

Everybody can get something out of learning to write better, think better, read better. I'm very honest and pretty critical. I'm not eager to be ingratiating, and I *may* say, "put that story away." I mean, I don't like to let a lot of futile work go by. But there are ways of doing it. You can say to someone, "Look, I just don't think your story is going anywhere," or, "I think you're becoming preoccupied with something that's more trivial than you thought." That's different from refusing to finish reading the story, or saying, "This is an example of tripe."

The other thing is, I let the students in my class talk more than I do. I very often feel they have a better sense of what's there than I do. Often, I'll hang back and it's the students who say the most cogent things about the writing. What I say at the end of most discussions is, "OK, Joe, Jane, you've heard all of this, take it home and figure out which of these comments tell you what you think you need to hear and ignore the rest of them. It's for you to decide." If everybody jumps on the writer and says, "I don't like that ending," you still want to turn to that writer and say, "If this is the ending you think you want, you've got a problem, because twelve people here aren't convinced by it. But if that's the ending you want, you keep it; it's your story. We'll try to help serve those needs by telling you what works and doesn't work."

The poet Marie Ponsot, who just retired from Queens College, is a brilliant teacher, by the way. She goes around the room and everybody contributes one sentence of uncritical observation: "It's a poem about the death of the heart" or "It's in trimeter." By the end, the writer is led to see what has emerged on the page, and what has not. That's an extreme example of returning the choice of what's important to the author, the class only deciding whether or not the work succeeds in showing it.

Q: I'd just like to touch on a question I also asked Stanley Elkin, namely, what it means to be called a "moral" writer. Philip Lopate, in his introduction to your reading at the 92nd Street Y last night, called you "our own Nadine Gordimer." What does that mean to you?

I'm not sure what it means to me, though I'm pleased if that's the way it comes out. I have a lot of trouble with a good bit of the fiction that's being written today, and it's not a question of taking a moral stand in the writing. In fact, if you look at a book like *Before and After*, you aren't really going to find *my* moral standards, just a presentation of some possible responses to hard questions. But one of the things I find absent from a lot of writing is a willingness to exercise analysis. A lot of what you read today—call it minimalist or whatever you want—to me reads like a film script. And I'm not original in saying this. Some of it can be interesting, but the thing I find lacking in so much of it is the thing a novelist can give us, which is complexity, drawing us into an understanding of what someone is thinking—not just showing how he acts. It's one of the things that my graduate students have a hard time understanding, being young contemporary readers. I remember giving them Elizabeth Bowen to read and they objected to it by saying, "She keeps telling us what to think. How *nineteenth century!*" She would say things like "Portia is a girl who. . . ." But I miss commentary. I miss intelligent, crafted, complex responses to characters and situations. I don't think it has to do with preaching what to think. It means that the person you meet on the page is not someone you're simply seeing frontally.

I suppose in my own fiction this is not something that I particularly set out to do, but the stories that interest me the most are the ones that try to take me behind our facades. I read somewhere that I was a meditative writer. News to me, but I like that. What I'm interested in and perhaps what I'm good at is watching the minds of my characters work. And that's what makes me the writer who seems, what, "moral." Not just watching what people do, but hearing people think, characters questioning themselves. That's very hard to do in a strictly minimalist story.

Q: One which Madison Bell described as composed of action, dialogue, action, dialogue, with never any exposition.

No exposition, no analysis, and no synthesis. And I miss it. I don't mind being called a nineteenth-century novelist. You can read *Civil Wars* slowly. Everything doesn't have to be read as quickly as a film script.

Q: Do you bring your preference into the classroom?

I don't know if I do it as often as I'd like to. But I remember an old teacher quoting Chekhov to us: "Help us walk into someone else's mind. . . . Look how you live, my friend." It's what I try to get my students to see. Don't judge your characters. You may want to set them up for your readers to judge, but don't savage them and don't make them look stupid, because what you're trying to do is understand what it feels like to be in their heads. Sometimes students don't want to hear that because it blunts their cleverness. It's easier to stand outside; more fun, too.

One of the failures of art is a failure of compassion, and that happened to me with my character Teddy, in *Civil Wars*. I don't think he works. Why would the woman, who is my major protagonist, have stayed married to him all this time? I just couldn't get the reader into his head sufficiently. Unlike Ben [in *Before and After*]. There are people who hate Ben, but I think I gave him a fair chance. You may or may not agree with or approve of him, but I think he gets to say his piece in a way that represents wholly how he wants to be judged; and he would say to you, "I'll take my chances." What I hope with my students is that somehow I can get across to them the moral dimension that says you've got to give everyone a fair shake. You don't have to love them, but they have to have a chance to be represented at their worst and at their best in their totality.

Q: Stanley Elkin spoke of good characters having an integrity, meaning a wholeness, a believability.

And some of his characters, goodness knows, are on the edge. They're not paragons, let's say. But he's right, that isn't the point. It doesn't mean you have to write about good people. In fact, I've excelled at writing characters people don't like. (I've often thought of writing a dissertation on unlikeable characters!) Some of Stanley Elkin's characters, such as Ed Wolfe in "I Look Out for Ed Wolfe," are not exactly guys you'd want to take home to Mama; but Ed Wolfe is there in his fullness and richness, and you know him. It's an artist's morality, not any other one, and those are characters we, their creators, often love the most.

Q: Where do you think your students fit in all this? They're young.

[Pause.] I don't know. Some of the cleverest of them are the worst offenders, still showing off. But I don't want this to sound as if I'm preaching a pollyanna approach for students or teachers. There's plenty of room among teachers with different points of view. What do you do when you have extremely strong views about something, some terrible offense given by society? Isn't there room for a suspension of neutrality? I've been talking about being morally neutral and giving everybody a chance to express whatever they feel. But I guess, again, that diversity should invite teachers of different kinds, and a program needs a little deeply felt bias as well. It's probably quite useful for students to have examples before them of teachers who are passionate about something, and that may make them unfair about other things. It's not bad to have all these kinds of models, approaches.

Generally, I think the major problem my students have is the triviality of what engages them; many of them are in love with those tiny little stories. Rather than engaging large questions, they're really looking at young people like themselves, doing odd jobs, people who don't have careers or directions. Like early Anne Beattie stories. It's a kind of solipsistic writing.

I remember when I read this book called *Twenty Under Thirty* a few years back, the best of the stories were by people who actually *dared* to write as other people, distant from themselves. It works so much better than when they try to be themselves adrift in their generation, which is an easier story to write because you don't have to learn about something else.

Also, as far as I'm concerned, the main thing undergraduates have to learn is how to read. Often they're not sophisticated readers. The best thing any undergraduate said to me about my class was that "I can't go to the doctor's office anymore and pick up *Ladies' Home Journal* and read one of those stories and be satisfied. You taught me there were better things than that." That's probably one of the most useful things a teacher can do. You want to educate readers to take literature seriously.

As for graduate students, one of the painful things is that so many of them do not go on to write, even the good ones; and you can't legislate that, *will* them to love it, to rethink their choices of priorities. But what's painful to me is the reason: money. I didn't work much of the time and my husband was a public school teacher, so for a very long time we didn't have very much money (though I always made sure we had baby-sitters or day care for my kids so that I could write, because that was a priority). So I do tend to get a little self-righteous with my students. But a lot of them don't fight for their writing when they think they can't make enough money doing it. And I say, "You don't *need* so much of what you think [you do]." They don't *need* clothes that cost what they cost, the most expensive dish on the menu, the car. But they don't see that as a choice, or they're really tired of living close to the bone, and many of them end up dropping out after they've finished the program because they think they need to take good jobs.

But I think if they looked at their "necessities" with a really hard eye, they'd stay lean for the fight and be writers.

Nicholas Delbanco

Nicholas Delbanco, born in 1942, was six when his family moved from London to Larchmont, New York. By his own account of his apprenticeship, he wanted to be either "poet, folk-singer or movie star" when he signed up for a fiction workshop one summer at Harvard. The results were immediate. "The first word I wrote for Updike was the first of my first novel." It was the only workshop Delbanco ever took, perhaps the only one John Updike ever gave; and *The Martlet's Tale* was published with fanfare in 1966.

Nine more novels followed by the time he was thirty-seven, including his "Sherbrookes trilogy," and they were followed in turn by works as diverse as *About My Table, and Other Stories* (1983), *The Beaux Arts Trio* (1985), *Running in Place: Scenes from the South of France* (1989), and most recently *The Writers' Trade and Other Stories* (1990).

The year his first novel appeared, at the age of twenty-three, Nicholas Delbanco also went to replace Bernard Malamud as a teacher at Bennington College, where he stayed for nearly twenty years and cofounded, with John Gardner, the Bennington Writing Workshops. He has been a visiting professor at the University of Iowa, Williams College, Skidmore College, Columbia University, and the Bread Loaf Writers' Conference. Currently, he directs the graduate writing program at the University of Michigan.

It is thus from the perspective of virtual child prodigy in two fields, writing and teaching, that Delbanco speaks here about the shifting shape of the writer's career and of the constant need, as artist, to change and to replenish. Of teaching itself he has said, "I love a chance to be in the presence of great language and to address it out loud, and to be in the presence of those who dream of producing great language and be witness to that growth."

The University of Michigan, in Ann Arbor, offers a B.A. in English and a two-year M.F.A. in Creative Writing, poetry or fiction. This conversation took place in New York City.

Q: You've described learning to write fiction as an apprenticeship, with "stages" that "seem at the least confusing; it is not a mere matter of time" [from "Judgment: An Essay," in Writers on Writing, *1991]. But the notion of apprenticeship seems almost an odd one at a time when writers in their twenties produce best-sellers. What does it really consist of, this apprenticeship to writing?*

Well, as I said in that piece, the model of the medieval guild is a very useful one for me. After a period of learning, the writer receives a kind of walking paper that permits him to pose as a journeyman-laborer and enter the guild; then, ideally, he has the chance of becoming a master craftsman and having people report to *him*. In many ways that's a model that pertains to writing programs, where students of the craft come to learn it at the hands or feet of someone who is reputedly a master craftsman. Or, more properly, crafts*person*.

Now, that analogy breaks down of course as soon as you look at it a little more closely. First, it's pretty difficult to declare that anyone *is* a master craftsman, able to turn one's hand to whatever piece of work is commissioned. Well, George [Garrett] might come damn close, in that he does seem to be able to do nearly everything. I'm pretty obviously a journeyman-laborer of some attainment by now, but when does one say, "Oh, now the person has attained a mastery and can pass it down?" The first master craftsmen that come to mind are not necessarily authors. I think [cellist Pablo] Casals in his great old age was probably a master teacher; there are master painters, master choreographers. This is a rather common model, in a sense, of the person who exemplifies artistic attainment. And that has something to do with the pleasure I think that most writing students take in an "eminent" teacher, being in the presence of someone who has practiced the craft proficiently.

But it gets complicated. An athletic coach does not necessarily have to have been a better athlete than the person he or she is coaching; a vocal coach is very often a failed performer; and some of the great teachers of the violin, say, need not have been great violinists. So it's not clear to me that the best writers are the best teachers. It may be wonderfully invigorating to be in the presence of X, Y, or Z whose work you admire, but you may get nothing from them in class. And it may be dispiriting to be in the presence of someone whose work you have either never read or liked, yet that person may be perfectly able to allow you to find your own voice and attain your own walking papers.

Q: Let me ask you to break it down even further. In your essay you write that "we must work through derivation, toward the original voice," and in your book Running in Place: *"How else does one acquire earned originality than by influence absorbed?..." How important is imitation of the teacher, say, in the path to writing?*

Where do I think that happens, and when?

Q: And how long should it go on?

Well, this is another reason my original model breaks down. If you're in somebody's carpentry shop, you're supposed to be able to learn how to replicate their chest of drawers or their trestle table—you're supposed to get as close to the master's originating form as possible. Reubens in his atelier had apprentices so good that they could do the dog or the foot or even the face without the master having to supervise. All of this "school of . . . " or "from the workshop of. . . ," all those models are perfectly appropriate when you're talking about craft; they're *not* so appropriate when you're talking about art.

My notion of a failed writing workshop is when everybody comes out replicating the teacher and imitating as closely as possible the great original at the head of the table. I think that's a mistake, in obvious opposition to the ideal of teaching which permits a student to be someone *other* than the teacher. Not everyone who gets walking papers into the guild should walk with the same gait or produce the same trestle table: The successful teacher has to make each of the students a different product rather than the same.

And that's another reason why it's problematic to establish a model, because there are so many different varieties. I taught Bret [Easton] Ellis, for instance, when he came to Bennington [College]. In many ways his work was fully formed in his first workshop. I don't mean that he didn't work very hard at honing the craft and that he won't continue to need to do so in the years and decades to come, but he had his own established voice already. Another student of mine from the old Bennington days, a fellow called Ted Mooney, who was easily as gifted, was full of changeable vocalics, so that you never quite knew what his voice was going to be. It took him I would say eight years or so upon graduation to produce his first novel, which was called *Easy Travel to Other Planets*, whereas Bret seemed to have a "style" early on. I don't think there's any intrinsic hierarchy here, or that the one is any better than the other. The problem with a writing program and writing class is that the verdict ain't in when the grade arrives. By this I mean, when you graduate from business school or law school or medical school, you have a very good sense of the shape of your career. For a young writer, however, it can take two, five, seven, twelve years before the verdict is in, and that's very difficult to equate with the notion of professional training.

Donna Tartt was a Bennington student and seemed to labor in obscurity for seven or eight years while Jill Eisenstadt and Bret and people like that were taking stage center. She seems to have come out of that obscurity, rather, hasn't she? I just think it's a mistake to try to predict how long it will take an author to find a voice or even, come to that, to assume when you find a voice for a first book, the second or third will necessarily replicate it or remain.

Q: Do writing programs, then, presume too much? Are they too bound up in producing published writers now rather than opening up students for the long road ahead? Or does everyone know it's a long road all along?

What I certainly say to our entering graduate students at Michigan is that we can guarantee close attention for a couple of years to the skills of the craft and the problems posed, but can't guarantee, goodness knows, that there'll be publication or a pot of gold at rainbow's end. It's dishonest to predict that concomitant with the M.F.A. will come a career. It would presume too much, like the old writers' courses that you sent away for, to promise professional attainment at curriculum's end. I guess there's a way that certain programs advertise themselves as tickets to fortune and fame; but I don't think anyone actually says that more than subliminally.

Q: The marketplace is at least in the back of students' minds. You yourself published out of college and you'd written ... how many books by the age of—what?

I guess I'd published ten novels by the time I was thirty-seven.

Q: An extraordinary number.

Well, in some sense it was very fortunate—I was very glad I got all those books out of my system and onto the shelves. In another sense, though, and to return to your first question, I think I felt that, oh, anyway the first five or six were technically apprentice works.

Q: In that case, hypothetically of course, would it be better to have no marketplace at all staring at very young writers of twenty-one, twenty-two? To give them a chance to develop without it?

My first novel came out when I was that age in 1966, and it really was a success, a large success in certain terms. On the day of publication the Sunday *New York Times* praised it lavishly; the daily *New York Times* weighed in that week. I mean, I can't remember the dates and places of reviews, but my picture was in a lot of magazines, the book got reprinted, a movie was made, and if nothing else it guaranteed the publication of my next two or three books. So by the time it was over I had a career. And in that sense I was the then-contemporary precursor of [Jay] McInerney or Ellis or Tartt or who-have-you. But the terms of the proposition then were totally other. No matter how successful I was at that moment, I had nothing like the success that these young writers are having today, because now, especially relatively recently, young writers are treated the way rock stars are, or famous young athletes. What my first novel provided me was a few thousand dollars, the ability to tell my anxious parents that in fact I was a writer, and it probably got me a job—though in fact I learned later that my colleagues at Bennington were more inclined to give me a job *before* they read the book than after!

So the sort of early success that I had was in no important way life-changing. What it allowed me to do was continue to write. I do think that the great American dream-and-fame-and-commerce machine has come dangerously into play of late, and that young writers now are at much greater risk than those of my generation of becoming cultural icons. And replaceable for that reason.

There's a wonderful phrase in a wonderful book by Cyril Connolly, *Enemies of Congress*. While warning of the dangers of success, he declares, "The best thing that can happen for a writer is to be taken up very late or very early, when either old enough to take its measure, or so young that when dropped by society he has all life before him." And elsewhere he announces, "Young writers, if they are to mature, require a period of between three and seven years in which to live down their promise." [Laughs.]

I think early publication, though its benefits are obvious, has some not-too-obvious, very real risks.

Q: To get back to the question of imitation, given the particular commercial advantages of success now, do you tend to see students imitating their older, successful teachers; or is what you see something of the opposite, writers trying to strike out with individual voices, regional voices, New Age or slick or whatever kinds of voices?

Well, even though regional voices are imitative often—there are probably twenty people in North Carolina who would love to be Lee Smith right now, twenty in Montana who want to be Richard Ford—still, one tends to flatter by imitation. There's nothing wrong I think with admiring writers and wanting to sound somewhat similar to them. The risk of course is when the imitation grows slavish or when the originality ain't there in the first instance, and so you get lots of little Nabokovs or Carson McCullers. It doesn't much matter *what* the model, to pattern yourself after it slavishly is hardly a serious way to attain an independent voice. In a world that I don't know very well, the world of contemporary music, it seems to me that a lot of people replace each other in rapid commercial succession, and that it's the rare performer who outlasts a generation or a decade. And I suppose there's some risk of that in writing, too.

Ray Carver, for instance, who was I think a genuine original, did spawn quite a few and far too many folk in his mode. I suppose Tom [T. Coraghessan] Boyle is doing something like that today. Lots of people this week want to write a "Tom Boyle" sort of story. If they're good they'll get beyond it, and if they're not, probably not much damage has been done. I don't think it's a high-risk proposition.

I think really, and this is the long answer to your impressively short question, I think really that the best writing teacher in the history of the enterprise has not created a silk purse from a sow's ear, has not been able to confer genius on a student who didn't have it, and the worst writing teacher in the history of the enterprise—although this is a little harder to prove—the worst writing teacher has probably not wrecked genuine talent. I mean, I suppose it's possible that some little Herman Melville went to X program and met Y teacher and said, "I'm never going to write again," and an incalculable loss to American letters ensued. I tend to doubt it; I don't think really bad writing teachers have destroyed really good writers. So what we're talking about, then, is a very limited enterprise. If you can't keep a good man or woman down and if you can't create one where they didn't *a priori* exist, what we're talking about is in effect helping young talent once you identify it, or when it declares itself in your presence. And *that* I think is an honorable role and one we should all celebrate. John Updike played that role for me.

Q: And yours was the only writing class he ever taught, wasn't it?

My great claim to contemporary American fame may be that I drove him kicking and screaming from the academy! But he served wonderfully for me, as sort of an exemplary instance of a working writer. He has been my teacher in a certain sense ever since. And whenever we're in touch, which we are by letter quite often, or even when I review his books, which I have of late, I still feel a deferential, apprentice-to-master relation. And it's not because he's taught me anything much specifically in the last twenty years or so. Nonetheless, he was there to ratify the fact that I write. And that mattered to me enormously. In the same sense, I have a student named Andrea Barrett—do you know her work? Well, she's somebody I picked out of a class in Bread Loaf eight or nine years ago and her fourth novel is about to appear [*The Forms of Water,* 1993]. We don't see each other much, but I think I will probably always serve as teacher to her. And it's not really that I taught her anything she wouldn't anyway know, or discovered someone no one else would have recognized. It's just that there's that small category I was talking about, the real talent that declares itself and that you can say, "Oh, yeah, I maybe can save you a little bit of time by suggest-

ing a procedure, a way to cut through this Gordian prose-knot."
And that as I said is a very limited but an honorable and an
actual task.

*Q: Not to be too psychoanalytic about it, but does the student inter-
nalize that model of the teacher, of nurturance, and carry it with
him or her?*

I think so. As I'm further removed from the age of my students and sit there slumping in my chair at the head of the
table, I more and more remember my own masters, my own
school instructors, people who looked down on me from what
seemed like an insuperable height. In fact, some of my most
important experiences of being a young writer consisted of having gone to hear old writers who I admired, presences on the
podium.

*Q: Well then, let me ask you about George Garrett, whom you've
known and been a colleague of. Is his model of teaching, which is
rather an open, embracing model, similar to yours?*

Honestly I don't quite think so. I mean, I revere George this
side of idolatry, and I think he has written several of the masterpieces of our time and been a wonderfully successful teacher.
His roster of students is very impressive, and he probably has—
and this is a real measure—more books dedicated to him than
any other American author. I mean, he's a bloody hero. But he
does tend to teach with a sort of blanket enthusiasm and encouragement, and you have to know him awfully well to distinguish
the person he takes seriously from the person he doesn't,
because he's so gentlemanly and so courtly.

I'm a little tougher-minded, a little less of an all-embracing
witness in the classroom. I'm not sure which style yields more
or more rapid results.

*Q: There will always be a personality difference between any two
teachers, I suppose.*

That's right. Someone like Stanley Elkin, or even more so his now-dead colleague Howard Nemerov, who was my colleague at Bennington way back when, operates on precisely the reverse pedagogical notion. Which was that the *real* writer could not be discouraged, and that you were doing the profession a favor by discouraging everybody, under the assumption that a very small proportion of them would endure. I fall somewhere between those two models, George's and Howard's. It's tricky. If there's someone in the room with no talent, I tend to offer some encouragement, saying, "Oh, that's much better, wonderful, you know, look how much better you are now than three months ago, that's terrific." And if there's a student whom I take seriously and who I think really is gifted, I tend to say to him or her that they're wasting my time, they should pull up their socks, go home, and do it again—in other words I'm much tougher on the better students, kinder to students I don't find interesting. And that's a paradox the better students learn to comprehend.

Q: And future students who read this will know exactly where they fall!

That's true! Oh, God.

Q: The role of the mentor, whether as an actual or emotional presence, brings me to ask you about John Gardner. First of all, you started the Bennington Writing Workshops with him. Was there a model for that summer program originally, or did it just pick up and go?

John had already by then been teaching at Bread Loaf for quite a long time. I've been teaching at Bread Loaf for quite a long time since, and I suppose in one way or another I went there to replace him after his death. Bread Loaf was organized around the justifiable assumption that people spend most of their year working on projects in isolation, and that what they ought to do when they get there is not bring a typewriter, not do any writing, but rather listen to other people's talks, go to readings and lectures, get responses on their [previously written] manuscripts, and then go back the other fifty weeks of the year and work. Well, although this system has its real merits, it had gotten on John's nerves a little bit and was contrary also to my notion of what such an experience should be.

We were being asked and paid to look at work that an author himself [might not have] looked at for a decade. So we got into the notion of the workshop being the *work shop*, where you came in, you start to write, and people respond hot off the press. In fact we rather consciously said, "We're going to run a new summer workshop at Bennington that lasts a month, and you're going to have to bring a typewriter and you have to give us revisions, and what we want to look at is not old work but work you are doing at the present moment." The notion wasn't sit back and ruminate upon your work or that of others, it was: produce it. And that was a clear pedagogical bias on our part, and all else followed. . . .

Those were the years when John and I were in each other's pockets all the time, going back and forth on a daily basis as to the theory and practice of art. I don't think when we started it ever occurred to us that the writing workshops would become such a long-lived and substantial enterprise. It was just, "Wouldn't it be fun to talk about this stuff together and in the presence of a dozen students or so?" which is what we had that first year. And we got people like John Cheever and Bernard Malamud to come in, because they were around and willing, and obviously it just took off.

Q: Gardner, with his writing books, has become a kind of guru for many people who are unable to reach a workshop—even though he's no longer alive.

Well, as you probably know, I'm his literary executor and therefore responsible for the republication of his books. It's no surprise to me, but it's really interesting to register, that what seems to have been the enduring effect of his work—though I don't think the verdict is finally in—has to do with pedagogy, particularly *The Art of Fiction* but to a degree also *On Becoming a Novelist*. Those are works that almost everybody seems to have on their shelves, as writers.

Q: In these interviews I've been quoting Gardner occasionally as a stimulus, and what seems to happen is that people take off in criticism of something he said.

Well, Stanley [Elkin] was furious—and I don't think George [Garrett] got along with him all that well either. I loved John, but he was an irascible figure.

Q: In On Becoming a Novelist, *Gardner wrote: "Nothing is second hand: what [the promising writer] offers he has taken from life experience, not from Faulkner or, say, Kojak." I want to ask you about life experience in a moment, but first, what about books? Can they be mentors, too, in a sense?*

The common denominator of all writers, I believe, is a deep and abiding love of reading. That doesn't mean you have to have a doctorate or even a college degree; it doesn't mean you have to have read deeply in the classics or the faddish. It just means that all writers love to read. I simply don't believe that anyone who wants to enter this trade could have that desire until and unless they had a prior love and admiration of it through the act of reading. Anyway, I'm offering truisms. I don't think there's any canon one has to insist an author absorb; I do think that all authors have read widely if not well. And that very entry into other people's worlds is likely to shape to some degree the exploration of your own. And I don't see anything wrong with that.

Q: It's probably unavoidable.

Yeah. I mean, I'm no longer easily impressionable but I've just read the work of an author I hadn't really paid much attention to before and have been marvelously *impressed* by it—I'm referring to William Trevor. I just for instance reviewed eleven hundred pages of the collected stories; they are works of masterful authority. I would love to feel some of Trevor creep into Delbanco hereafter. And in a certain sense it would be fair to expect this, because he's now become an important part of my world, even though I've never met him and probably never will. And yet his way of looking at the world will have infected or inflected mine. Now, how enduring that will be or how much it will matter, these are other questions. But the notion that one is available to influence is, I suppose, another way of saying one is still alive and sentient. To try to be those people on whom nothing is lost, as [Henry] James famously observed, is to permit yourself to notice something. And if you're a bookish type one of the things you will notice is a book.

Q: And what about the concept of using life experience in writing? Stanley Elkin was fairly adamant in saying he didn't think young writers should write from experience, that they didn't yet know enough about themselves. For some students in M.F.A. programs, their life up to the age of twenty-five has been mainly a student life. Do you see students relying on their own, more narrow scope of experience instead of, say, working to develop an imaginative world?

Well, a couple of things to say about that. First—and since I would like to say this at some stage, I might as well say it now—we have a wonderfully good writing program at Michigan. We are able to be extremely rigorous in our selection process and take only the students we think are splendidly talented, and we've been proved right of late. Most of my students are now publishing to beat the band. Daniel Lyons, for example, just won both the AWP short fiction contest and the *Playboy* contest.

Every so often we take someone very young, but I do tend to want (and this is the first part of the answer) people who've got some experience of the world other than the time between the June they graduated from college and the September they matriculated into the program.

But I think equally important, and worth stressing, is the assertion that though young writers tend to think that the world will come to an end, and a happy one, when their first book appears, in fact all that means is that you now have your second one to write. It's not as if this is a game of tic-tac-toe, and once you figure out how to play it you can always get it right. It's process, isn't it, at least as much as result. . . .

And therefore the procedure and process of being a writer is a lifelong one. I mean, I've got fifteen books to my credit and I wake up every morning still wondering whether the hell I've got anything worth saying this morning, or whether I've lost it entirely or in fact ever *had* it. And I would warrant that Nobel laureates wake up with the same question. This is not a question that ever gets sufficiently answered, or if answered in the affirmative once, that doesn't mean it will be the next time it is asked. So it doesn't bother me that a young writer writes a "young writer's" book.

For instance, Donna Tartt's first novel [*The Secret History*] is a first novel. It's very nice that she's making so much money off it and that so many people are reading and buying it, but God help her if that's the best work she does. Right? And one of the risks, of course, of the fame that attaches to this publicity mill we mentioned earlier is that in fact you *are* encouraged to replicate rather than change and improve. I worry about that for Bret, for instance. It's quite possible his career is behind him already, which would be outrageous. I don't tend to think so, because he's got resilience and he's very young, and he may be in that category I referred to earlier, the writer who, when success deserts him, starts his career thereafter. Nonetheless, the point is that one writes in stages and in sequences, and it seems proper to me that when you are a young writer you write about a young writer's experience.

Q: It seems in every review of a young writer's book, there's that line, "This is the first work and we look forward to a maturing vision. . . ," which seems an obligatory thing to say—but on the other hand, there is an obvious truth to it.

The terrible opposite truth about American writers' lives is that the first book *is* quite often the most interesting—that something has evaporated, some obsession has been diminished, and that once you become a writer who is habitually at his or her desk, the originating wonder will be transmuted into mere professionalism.

And I think it fair to say that some of our great authors—Hemingway perhaps most notably—did their best work early. First, or virtually first. When your model is that of an athlete, say, and if you think of American writing as a prizefight with one available heavyweight champion—or as a kind of Superbowl with members of the winning team garnering the Pulitzer—you're pretty much foredoomed to think that age entails weakness and loss. In this paradigm you fail to improve as you work; you lose both your muscle and nerve. For obvious reasons, however, I prefer to think of different models—and they're ones I've proposed to you this morning—in which we equate age with growth. And that's another reason for this notion of a guild—of why we look up to our teachers, and what we as writers *profess*.

R.H.W. Dillard

R.H.W. Dillard was born in Roanoke, Virginia, in 1937. He attended Roanoke College, where he began his teaching career, and then the University of Virginia, where he received his Ph.D. at the age of twenty-seven. Since 1964 he has been professor of English and, since 1971, director of both the undergraduate and graduate programs in creative writing at Hollins College, in Roanoke, "serendipitously," he writes, "landing me right back where I literally began."

For a small program associated with a small, single-sex college, Hollins under Dillard has produced an astonishing number of good writers. Fred Chappell has said, "Sometimes one begins to think that the faculty and graduates of Hollins College supply half the world's books. Certainly they supply many of the best ones." Pulitzer Prize winners Annie Dillard and Henry Taylor are graduates of the program, as are Madison Smartt Bell, Tama Janowitz, David Huddle, and Lee Smith. Nevertheless, Dillard attempts to keep the program, with one of the highest publishing records of any graduate school in the country, "nonhierarchical" and "supportive," priding himself on the absence of a Hollins house style. "We do not really teach creative writing," he has said. "We do not produce writers who write a certain way. We provide the guidance of professionals and do everything we can to make the program what the students need."

As a writer of great freedom and experimentation, R.H.W. Dillard has produced four volumes of poetry, two novels (*The Book of Changes*, 1974, and *The First Man on the Sun*, 1983), two critical studies, a screenplay (*Frankenstein Meets the Space Monster*), and, most recently, a volume of collected stories called *Omniphobia* (1993). He is also the spirited creator of the Hollins film program, part of "the fun of a small school."

Hollins College offers a B.A. in English with a concentration in Creative Writing, and a one-year M.A. in English and Creative Writing. This conversation took place at Hollins College after an Advanced Creating Writing seminar, where graduates and undergraduates together discussed both their poetry and prose.

Q: The Hollins program is an unusual one, by all accounts. Small, but producing an extraordinary number of good writers. Tell me how it began.

A man named Louis D. Rubin, Jr., started the program. He came here in the late fifties with this funny idea that he could run a graduate writing program at a small liberal arts college for women. And it turned out to be an idea of absolute brilliance. He had written a novel, was a big-shot critic of Southern literature, had a newspaper background, and had the Johns Hopkins M.A. program as a model. He later wrote an article attacking graduate education, asking, "Why is it that you come out of a graduate education and no longer care for literature, no longer talk about the things that really matter?" So he just came up with this idea and Jack Everett, the college president at the time, was a forceful enough guy that even though a lot of the faculty didn't approve—BAM—it went in.

It was very small at first. One student! But they had the good luck to have William Golding here as writer-in-residence the year *Lord of the Flies* hit. So they got publicity, got in *Esquire*. Lee Smith and Annie Dillard came here as freshmen, primarily to study with Golding, and it went steadily upward. The numbers, however, increased real slowly. When I got here in '64 there were three grad students. When I was acting director in '67/'68 I got it up to seven. George [Garrett] came and was director for three years and he pushed it up to nineteen. Then the school panicked and squeezed it back down to twelve.

I was the bargain-basement director. They interviewed all these big shots to come in and run it, but when the subject of salary came up they turned back to me and said, "You do realize, don't you, that it was you all along!"

Q: Well, you were young for a director of a program.

I was something like twenty-seven when I got here, thirty-one when I became director. Like the turtle, you know, once I get hold of something I never let it go. People say, "You've been working here for twenty-nine years, did it ever occur to you to leave?" I say, "What are the odds anyone else would ever hire me?" [Laughs.]

Well, now of course it's different. The grad program has stabilized at sixteen. And there's a huge number of undergraduates here who study creative writing, roughly 140 out of 800, a big percentage, and they can do it every semester and every year.

Q: *The central question is: Why? What are the reasons for the success? You say it happens that there's been a crescendo of good people coming through, but there must be a philosophy that attracts them, too.*

Oh, yeah. There are theories about why it works. But I hate to talk about it. [Whispers.] I was always told you shouldn't brag.

Q: *Go right ahead.*

Well, the reasons are so obvious that nobody believes them. It's the idea of the community of writers, small so everybody knows each other, large enough so it's not hothouse small. I think the method—and there is a sort of Hollins method but it does sound awfully self-regarding when you describe it—the central effort is to encourage people to write the best they can the way *they* write. That is, not to impose a house style. It's so simple, and yet a lot of schools don't do that. In our recent anthology, *Elvis in Oz* [1992], you can see it. People just don't sound like each other. In order to do that, you can't use the model a lot of schools use, the model of master–pupil, where the work is presented to the class and then the teacher tells the class what's right or what's wrong and then you go on to the next one.

Last night, for instance, you saw that I rambled on too long at the beginning because everyone was nervous with you in the room—and on occasion I do that anyway, go into a kind of fugue state!—but no one is ever going to say, "This is how I would have written this story." Instead they're going to say, "I think I understand what you're doing, and I think if you do *this* it will be better in terms of what you are trying to do." And a kind of nice mutual respect develops. We've had people visit here as writers-in-residence who have grown up on the other model and they can't really believe what's happening. It seems chaotic: "Where's the line here, where's the control, where's the truth?" they ask.

Well, the truth's all over the place. We have students commenting in writing on each other's work, and when you read through a dozen comments on your poem or story, ten of them are probably irrelevant. But with a little luck, two of them are going to tell you *just* what it was you needed to know.

There's something else we do as well, which makes us seem soft to many people. We always try to keep the atmosphere positive rather than negative. I learned early on that if you come down real hard on the work of someone who's young and sensitive—and maybe old and insensitive, too—you often are going to crush them right there; they aren't going to write anymore. Well, a lot of people say there are too many writers anyway, and if they're not strong enough to take the heat they should get out of the kitchen. But you can tell the same truth in a supportive way without crushing people. And writers can be rough on each other.

Q: Going back to the first part of the equation, how do you step out of the master–pupil loop, given that you are, after all, their teacher?

Two things come to mind right off. A great part of the class is that students do the teaching. I'm on vacation. I'm sure everyone in their hearts thinks it's because I'm a lazy bum, and I also never write comments on the work turned in. I'll talk to people for an hour about a poem or a line, but I learned that what students tend to do if the teacher includes his own written comments in a stack of student comments is leaf through and find the one with the teacher's—and that automatically puts them back into the master–pupil model. People who are new to the class sometimes say to me, "Which one of these comments is yours, I don't know your handwriting?" And I'll say, "Well, why do you want to know that?" They say, "It's the one that really matters." And that's exactly why I don't give it.

Q: Isn't it natural, though, that some students yearn for the strong hand? Some of Gordon Lish's students told me—he did, too, actually—that some students can't take the heat and don't make it, while others are guided by an authoritative voice and thrive.

Well, I don't know if people who need the strong hand *really* need it, because what they turn into is Lish clones, who learn how to write a certain kind of sentence, a certain kind of story. Well, let *him* write that. Sometimes you go through a stage in your development when you need somebody to say, "No, this is dead wrong, believe me, do this right now." They'll come and talk to me and I'll tell them what I think—but only with the understanding that mine is another opinion. If I really feel that the class discussion got way off the base, I'll try and tell them, *"From my experience*, don't pay much attention to that."

Last night you saw the Advanced Creative Writing, a seminar of advanced undergraduates and some graduates, too. There, your real job is to talk *well* about other people's work. We have another course in which only the graduates, four at a time, are grouped with a faculty member. The first few weeks everyone is stiff and scared. We have flare-ups and quarrels. But they really bond and get so good at reading each other's work that by the end I almost don't have to say anything. I drop in and watch. My theory is that most of what you learn as a student comes from talking about other people's work. You can get such a mixed collection of comments on your own work it's sometimes hard to sort it through.

So you work differently in each situation. One is much more open and varied, the other can be real direct, with people who know your work from the inside every time. It's good to get both of those things.

Q: Some of your former students told me directly, and Madison Bell said it indirectly, that their one year at Hollins gave them a chance to find their own voices. Is that a goal?

You cross your fingers and hope that's what happens. With novelists turning in their drafts, what you almost have to do is resist the urge to fix anything too quickly. Let it grow for a while. Then all of a sudden everyone will see what went wrong, if it did. It's risky but better sometimes to let them make their own mistakes; they build on it, they talk to each other—and it gets transformed as it goes. So Madison got to work on *Washington Square Ensemble* and by the spring he was really rolling; he had the voices. Tama Janowitz said the same thing. Tama had no background in creative writing, and she didn't have a great year here, for a number of reasons. But nevertheless she honors the place because this is where she got to write her first novel. She found her way.

Of course, what she and other people may worry about is that sometimes they feel they're not getting the kind of criticism they thought they would. When you let them go and wait a while, sometimes they say, "Why bother to come to the place at all if no one's going to tell you anything?" [Laughs.]

But you have places where people get real writer's block, get spooked because everyone else is cranking it out so much faster and more securely. Here, Madison and Jill McCorkle were in the same class and were writing at such speed it was scary. Madison wrote a novel, Jill a novel-and-a-half. What it did to the other students in that group, however, was get them writing faster too. We had enormous amounts of work done.

Q: There is another dimension to talk about. Another of your former students, Adam Ross, said that you helped him not only to write but to "see."

Now you've got me where I can't answer. Maybe it's because . . . oh, yeah, he took my film course! He took my Hitchcock film course. Often that will help fiction writers better than a novel course. It's a different way of telling narrative in which you have no choice literally but to *see* what's going on.

Q: You also teach a course called, "Film as Narrative Art." What's going on there?

Nowadays what I do is teach single directors, but it's evolved over twenty years. We look at films and see how they're put together. How does this image tell the story, whereas if you just read the script you don't have the story? I think that's good for fiction writing because it forces you out of your normal mode of thinking. You bring it back your own way.

One thing a fiction writer learns in film is that the story is not told by the plot. The story is told by the whole texture in which the plot participates. On their own they start thinking about their novels and they realize the same thing, that the *language* tells the story, that it's the equivalent of the visual image. The richness or plainness of the language is where the real action is.

Q: Last night, without hitting people over the head, you seemed to ease them into a different understanding of one of the stories under discussion. You helped them identify it, actually, as a fable, and that got the ball rolling. And the writer agreed with you.

I think you learn from experience. I didn't start teaching the way I teach now. I tended to think I knew it all. But I caught on fairly quickly that I didn't. It was a humbling experience. I would just blow it. Then I learned that the best thing to do if you just totally misread something is to confess it immediately: "Boy, was I stupid." Beyond that, some of it's intuitive, some you pick up. Last night I could tell that people were saying thoughtful things about the story but they wanted it to be something else. You just have to learn when to be rude and break in and shift the discussion. That's why I asked the writer what she wanted it to be.

Q: Alternately, you could have spent an hour going over the story editorially, without questioning what it really was you were editing.

In that case, working on details, I didn't think it would have worked. You know, "Did you really think this character would have been driving a Buick?" On the other hand, if the story is pretty intact and just needs line editing, and if you're confident the students read it the way it wanted to be read, then that's fine, let it go. And sometimes the class will resist when you try to step over and talk about the thing as a whole. They think I've just gone off to cuckoo-land. They do their Reagan imitation: "There he goes again." So if, in the ambience of a particular class, I can't bring in a larger issue, I just go back to line editing for a while and try to sneak it in somewhere else.

Q: Your undergraduates didn't seem at all intimidated by the graduates in the class, which was surprising.

Some students *are* intimidated. Some are worried. The graduates scare them. But after a few weeks, they're pros. Plus, especially after a year or so, the undergraduates have been through a crop of grad students the year before and know they're not that scary.

It works both ways, too. You can have a graduate who comes in with the big head and thinks he's in class with a bunch of bow-headed bimbos, until one of those bow-headed bimbos writes something that's so much better than he could write. It's a great experience, really good for him, humbling in the right way. Eventually, everyone starts finding his or her own level, starts making friends, and the ones who can talk at level A start talking at level A whether they're grad or undergrad.

When the program was created at such an unlikely place, part of the deal that was cut was that there would forever be a support to the undergraduates. That's one reason why this particular course is mixed. And I find it's very beneficial. Everyone has to learn to be more helpful, a little more patient, because sometimes someone is going to turn in something really bad and you just have to bring it along, find a nice way of saying, "Back to the drawing board."

Also, some people can take blunter kinds of remarks than others, and you just have to guess that, and sometimes you guess it wrong, you hit them too hard, or not hard enough. You also have to know that no one really wants what they claim to want. Once in a while students come to me to complain, and they say, "I know you're a nice man, and I know you're good-hearted, but you're simply not telling me the truth about this. You're not being honest." A woman once came to me who had applied to the grad program and been rejected, gotten her courage up and applied again. She was writing really good work, which went on to win an AWP prize the next year. She said she wanted the absolute truth. So I said, "All right. I didn't want to tell you but I will. The work you submitted two years ago when you applied was really third-rate. We didn't see any promise. The work you submitted the next year was better. The poems you're writing this year are terrific. You've clearly found out who you are and you're working well."

Crushed her. I didn't see her for a week. She later confessed she went home, sat alone in a darkened room, and got totally depressed. Even though what I told her was positive—"You weren't so good, now you're really good"—she didn't want it. So you always have to be careful.

Q: One of the benefits of keeping people writing, then, is that it allows them to find themselves, if not the year that they're here then maybe down the road?

It's an argument for this whole program. We're not going to make an effort to produce writers, but we're going to give people the opportunity to be better readers, better human beings. It so happened that this humane system produced writers at a pretty fast clip. There's something about coming in and knowing that in nine months you're out of here that works sort of subliminally to keep people very busy. They want to take advantage of every minute of it. We could shift it over and call it an M.F.A. and make it two years, but I think the one year somehow works.

Also, we get a goodly number of people who already have M.F.A.s and then come here. It goes both ways. They're buying another year. Or some of them say, "Well, I have my M.F.A. but I wanted to have *the Hollins experience*." I cringe. It makes it sound like a country club! But I know what they mean by it. Some atmospheric thing—more likely human than supernatural—enables an awful lot of people to get a lot of work done in a circumstance that, one way or another, they remember as very important and a very nice time in their lives.

Q: Well, unofficially I guess, you also supply a kind of postgraduate support system. Graduates come back to read. You have the anthology.

They're very loyal to the school and generally very nice to each other as they go on in their careers. I didn't mention this back when we started, but the other word I would use when I talk of Hollins is nonhierarchical. It's one of the distinguishing characteristics of the program. We don't have a pecking order among the students, or among the faculty . . . as long as they know I'm at the top! [Laughs.]

Seriously, I think it's very important. I've talked to people at other schools who said that elsewhere you always knew you were in a certain group: There was this little group of writers who were better, then a middle group, then the bums down below. We sure work hard not to have that separation here, I think with some success. In our anthology we've tried to make it as open as possible. The big shots are in there, but the other folks are in there, too.

Q: Is there a danger to being too far removed from the commercial world?

Well, you don't want to teach publishing procedures. If you just get people writing well, they'll do OK. Some of them won't, too. I've had people who've written like angels and then stopped. Life had something to do with it and it breaks my heart. I've had other people who just plodded along and then suddenly did very well. They had that determination and they pushed right through.

Judy Hawkes started writing a gothic novel when she was an undergraduate here, and nineteen years later her first novel is published, *Julian's House*, which did really well. She became smarter, more sophisticated, better, better, and finally when she wrote it, it became a fine piece of work.

Q: What about the argument, one that Eve Shelnutt made to me, that it's incumbent upon programs to give students a sense of critical theory, too?

I think it's terrible. I think it works absolutely against you. I had a bunch of grad students who said, "OK, let's study theory in a tutorial called 'Form and Theory.'" So we got Terry Eagleton's book [*Literary Theory*] and finally decided that the best way to read that book was to consider it a novel. And we began to discuss the character of the narrator! We did a number on that guy.

I think theory works against the grain. It's fine if people want to do it, but imaginative work, artistic work, is essentially *conjunctive*. It is a drawing together of unlikely things. That's how the imagination works. Theory and analytical work, on the other hand, are *disjunctive*. It's all a matter of taking something apart.

Let the reader study theory. Leave the writers alone. You see writers getting theory-bound and buy into Marxist theory or feminist theory or structuralist theory or poststructuralist theory. They feel an obligation because of poststructuralist canon, say, to put things in their work for ideological reasons, and you just watch the work die, die. Any writer who looks back over his or her own work and looks at the places where they felt the pressure of the day to make some kind of theoretical statement can always see those poor poems or stories sitting there with a cancer growing in them. It's good for students to know theories are out there. Some writing students take to them easily and comfortably and it doesn't harm them a bit. Others it just makes them doubt their own gift.

Q: You do something else. You allow them to cross over from fiction to poetry.

Yeah, we're one of the few programs that doesn't segregate on that basis. Fiction writers sometimes say, "Oh, are we going to do *poetry*? I don't understand *poetry*." Meaning, "I don't understand slime mold!" There's something so dismissive. But it's so good for them to have to deal with language at the poet's level. Everyone on the faculty writes fiction *and* poetry.

Q: It's a criterion?

Once I caught on that this is what we're going to need, the hiring has to go that way. You have to have been there, as a teacher. You can be a good critic and a good theorist, but you're not going to know how this sentence happened to be next to that sentence unless you do it, too. I discover when I hire a really terrific poet that they are unable to talk about fiction. And the other way, too. There are so many writers around who write both, I make an effort in hiring to lean in that direction.

Q: And your applicants to the program? If you followed it from a purely idealistic point of view—completely nonhierarchical—anyone who wanted would be able to come!

[Laughs.] Well, we've got room for ten. So it's highly selective and almost impossible to know how to do it. Say we get a hundred and sixty applications, probably a hundred of those, you can tell, would do fine here. And beyond that it's almost like a mystical trance state. Who do you feel would benefit this place and also benefit *from* this place? It's not purely just on quality of writing, it's also a kind of intuitive feeling that this person would like it here.

Q: The traditional European model of teaching writing, needless to say, is different from the American. There, to generalize, their question might be not "Can writing be taught?"—maybe it can—but "Should it be? Why teach it?" Why not get yourself a job in journalism, find a mentor, read Evelyn Waugh, find your niche, and go about it that way?

Of course, lately the Europeans are beginning to buy into our programs, too. But certainly the history of literature shows you don't need writing programs. But the history of technology and invention shows you don't need other kinds of programs, either. My argument is, "It is a nice time in your life as a writer you wouldn't have had otherwise, so why don't we supply it?"

On the other hand, more and more writers feel—and I could feel it too as a writer—that all those competent writing schools are just plugging up the publishing channels, and "I can't be as famous and successful as I want because there're just too many other people." You feel it, you wish sometimes they would just go away so you could be on the cover of *Time*. But the world's changed and people haven't caught on yet. There are going to be lots more writers and the audience is going to be smaller— regional audiences or audiences for a certain type of writing— and we're probably not going to have T. S. Eliot again. It's been a long time since everyone agreed who the major living poet was, and I wonder if they ever will again.

Q: Even though we all have a need to be told who's "good."

Oh, sure. We read reviews. I remember a scholar came to U.Va. when I was there and predicted a world without major writers. It made me almost sick to my stomach. Not only because deep inside it wouldn't be Roethke, Lowell, and Dillard. But more that—what you were just saying—I wanted a place where I knew who the good ones were and I could read them with total confidence and belief. I was a true believer. I read a Hemingway book, and whether it was good or bad, I thought it was wonderful. And Faulkner meant so much to me as a kid. But I read him now and see he's not perfect. That was very upsetting to me, but I think the world with all its technological leaps forward is going to be very different.

There's this machine I was reading about the other day. Bookstores are eventually going to stop carrying books. They'll have this big machine—it already exists—and you can go in and tell them the book you want and the machine plugs into Data Central and prints your book and binds it with the kind of binding you choose. What it means is that all books will suddenly be in print again.

Q: And everyone's personal canon will be side by side with everyone else's? That's amazing.

Yeah. It's going to reshape education in ways I don't have the imagination to figure out. The machine costs about a million dollars now, so WaldenBooks has not bought too many yet. But it'll change publishing, of course. The publishers will still get the manuscripts, edit them, advertise them, but they will no longer have to worry about the warehouse. Everything will be on a computer somewhere.

Q: Doesn't that go back to what you were saying about not wanting to comment in writing on students' manuscripts? Once the words are in print they take on a certain weight of authority they didn't have before. It goes against your dislike of hierarchies, but maybe it's just natural, too. We all learn to rank.

"There's a natural aristocracy among men," Jefferson said. (And we know what a sexist remark that was!) A certain kind of hierarchy will always develop. Some people are going to stick with it, some will write better. That'll happen. Still, I never want to impose my view.

George Garrett had a lot to do with getting me out of my I-know-it-all mode, pointing out that when creative writing teachers grade on the basis of anything other than effort, they're really just exercising taste. There's no such thing as objective grading. It may seem anarchistic the way George does it, but it's true.

Of course, at a certain point taste does kick in. Then you have standards. Even if you say to yourself, "I don't like this story," you can know it's good. For instance, I'm an oddball in that my own writing tends toward metafiction. My students, however, are realist writers. So even though I encourage them to try to do everything—and it all flows with literary tides, stories switched over to present tense, shifting back, Southern stories—I stick with my realists and support them to the death.

But they all know I'd like to have Italo Calvino in my class!

Stanley Elkin

Stanley Elkin was born in New York City in 1930 and raised in Chicago. He attended the University of Illinois, where he received his B.A., M.A., and Ph.D. in English, and now teaches creative writing at Washington University in St. Louis. Called "one of America's great tragicomic geniuses" (Robert Coover), he won a 1982 National Book Critics Circle award for his novel *George Mills*, was nominated for National Book Awards for *The Dick Gibson Show* (1971) and *Searches and Seizures* (1973), and was a 1991 National Book Award finalist for *The MacGuffin*. Harold Brodkey has written that Elkin "is more serious than anyone now alive, which may mean that he is at times a better writer than anyone."

In the conversation that follows, Stanley Elkin speaks about the nature of the story, the virtuoso music of style, and the meaning of "moral" fiction, all within the context of learning and teaching writing. In a wheelchair now (with multiple sclerosis), he is nevertheless a teacher of palpable energy and acute attentiveness, as I witnessed in both the graduate writing seminar he conducted at home and the undergraduate fiction-writing class on the Washington University campus. If "Elkin-on-the-page is too immediate, too large, too good to try to learn from" (Brodkey again), Elkin-in-person and in-the-classroom is both pragmatic and wise, helping his students identify the story within their work, if needed, and "pointing out the beauties" in those stories whenever possible. It is not necessary to say that he is also, in person and in these pages, an immensely funny storyteller.

Many of Elkin's essays have been anthologized (e.g., *1990 Best American Essays*) and collected (*Pieces of Soap*, 1992). His latest book is a trio of novellas called *Van Gogh's Room at Arles* (1993). Stanley Elkin is a member of the American Academy and Institute of Arts and Letters.

Washington University, in St. Louis, Missouri, offers a B.A. in English and a two-year M.F.A. in Writing.

Q: In the days you were getting your doctorate in American litera-
ture, were you studying to be a writer, too—or had you been writ-
ing all along?

I've been writing since the year dot. Not very well, but I
wrote what I thought were stories and, when I had to declare a
major at the University of Illinois, I said I wanted journalism
because I thought that stories were published in newspapers.
This was how much I knew. A wonderful freshman comp
instructor who liked my work said, "I see you've got yourself
down as a journalism major; you shouldn't be in journalism, you
should be an English major." He came to me and I do what they
tell me.

Q: You didn't consider a writing program?

If writing programs existed when I went to school, there
weren't many. There was probably Stanford and the University
of Iowa. I certainly didn't know about them, and had I known
about them I wouldn't have attended them. But I had some very,
very good writing teachers at the University of Illinois, where I
got all my degrees, cradle to grave. One of them was named
Jerome Beaty, who was not I think himself a writer. The second
was George Scouffas, who was not a writer. The third was Randall Jarrell, who was of course a marvelous writer, primarily a
poet but a writer, too, of a marvelous novel called *Pictures from
an Institution* [1954]. Jarrell was visiting at Illinois one semester
and one semester only, and I was fortunate enough to have him.
He was one of the best teachers I've ever had in my life.

Q: Well, why?

Well, for one thing he didn't do anything called workshops!
As a matter of fact, the students never saw each other's stories,
nor did he discuss our stories in class. What we talked about in
class was Chekhov, Chekhov's stories. I read Chekhov's stories
until I was blue in the face. And at the end of the semester he

would meet with each of us once. On the first day he passed a sign-up sheet, and he had some dates and told us to write our names on the sheets that went by. I wrote my name for some-time late in April, 1955, it would have been. He said he would not talk about our stories and would have nothing to say about them until we saw him in the conference. We had no homework, except reading the Chekhov stories. And we wrote at our own pace and turned our stories in to him.

My appointment with him was on a Tuesday. I'll never forget this. I went to his office and knocked on the door and there was no answer. I waited around for another ten minutes and he didn't show up. I waited for another twenty minutes and he didn't show up. I was kind of hurt that he'd forgotten my appointment, since I'd had no feedback from him all semester, and I only had this one shot at him. That was my first reaction. My second reaction was that I was angry. So I did something no one ever did in those days. I called the professor at home and woke him up. I said, "Mr. Jarrell, my name is Stanley Elkin, I'm in your writing class, my appointment with you was to have been at ten o'clock."

"Oh, oh," he said, "I'm so sorry, Mr. Elkin. Where are you right now?" This is a pretty fair imitation of him; he had this high squeaky voice like a kid whose voice was changing. "Where are you right now?"

"I'm in the English building at a pay phone."

"Well, uh, do you know my car?"

"No."

"I drive a red Oldsmobile convertible, and if you'll just stand outside, I'll be right over and pick you up."

So I went outside and waited for him and indeed this guy drove up in a red convertible and said, "Mr. Elkin, would you come over. I can't get out of the car. You'll have to get in the front." The reason he couldn't get out of the car was that he was in his pajamas. And slippers. Indeed, I *had* awakened him. And the two stories I had written were on the bench seat between us, and he said, "Just get in and we'll drive around." Now, he had total recall. "You'll see if you turn to page twelve. . . ." And he just ripped me to shreds. And we drove around campus, around and around and around campus, in traffic and out of traffic, for the better part of an hour. And then we just turned off toward the cornfields. It's in farm country, Champaign-Urbana, and we drove down country lanes and over roads and he, well, just devastated my story.

Q: Your heart must have been sinking.

Well, it was sinking and exalted at the same time, because he had such total memory of the story; I'm sure he had a mnemonic mind. So finally he dumped me back at the English building. This was way towards the end of the semester. I don't think there was another class. And he posted grades. Of the twenty-five people in class there were only two A's; one was mine.

I saw him one last time at Illinois. He was walking along the corridor, and I said, "Excuse me, Professor Jarrell?"

"Yeesss?"

"My name is Stanley Elkin and I . . . "

"Yesss?"

"I see that you posted the grades."

"Uh huh."

"Well, it's just that, you know, you gave only two A's and I got one of them and I was rather surprised because you were so critical of the two stories I turned in."

"Yesss?"

I said, "Do you think, sir, that, since there were only two A's in the class, I got one, my name is Stanley Elkin, do you think that if I were to write not necessarily either one of these stories but some *other* story that perhaps some time if I were to work on them, not next month, not next year, not five years . . . my name is Stanley Elkin, there were two A's in class, I got one . . . that I could possibly, you know, perhaps, be *published*? Just one story and I'd regard myself as a writer. What do you think?"

And he shrugged and said, "I don't know." And that's what I tell my students when they ask me. "I don't know."

Q: But Jarrell was important to you?

Oh, indeed. He was a wonderful teacher.

Q: And no workshop.

No workshop at all. And to tell you truth—I know what you're going to ask—I find that with the workshop in combination with the tutorial—a direct, one-on-one method with no one else there and I can ask them what it is they think they're up to as a writer—I get tremendous results. But I think you need both. I think the kid has got to be kicked around in the workshop and *then* see me. I mean, I'm going to see this one student whose story you heard [in the undergraduate class] next Tuesday, and she'll get better. She wouldn't get better if she didn't have the chance privately.

Q: She was the one whose story didn't go so well. On the other hand, in the graduate seminar I saw, the results were quite the opposite. Those were wonderful stories. And your method is not at all like Jarrell's.

That's right. I use no text in class. First of all, to tell you the truth, I didn't like the Chekhov stories. I like his plays just fine, and maybe something's lost in the translation—I'm sure there is—but what I did like was the way Jarrell talked about them. And Jarrell was like many an eighteenth-century critic whose only obligation to the text was to point out the beauties—not, obviously, in the case of the two stories I turned in to him. But that's what he did with Chekhov. I mean, he never convinced *me*, but while I was listening to him he was right. So that's why I asked Miss X [in the graduate seminar] this morning how she had achieved such-and-such an effect. I was trying to point out the beauties.

Q: I'd like to ask you about your teaching by way of your writing, if you don't mind—your stories and your novels, because people are interested in both.

What people? Name their names! . . . You know, Howard Nemerov, who's now, alas, dead, had been here at Washington University since 1969. He had very little to do with the writing program, although he occasionally did teach the poetry workshop. But somebody once asked him to autograph a book. The man walked very nervously up to Howard and said, "Would you please autograph this book for me, Professor Nemerov?" And Howard said, "Yes of course my dear, but you know, it would be much more valuable if I didn't. It's probably the only copy of this that has *not* been signed. I know all my readers by name!" [Laughs.]

Anyway, as for me, I *hate* my stories.

Q: You hate your stories?

I hate my stories. I'm not a story writer, I'm a novelist, a novel writer. Although I *am* working on a story now for the first time probably since . . . well, the last story I wrote was a thing I *did* like, called "A Poetics for Bullies," and I wrote that at Smith [College] in, let's see, 1964. . . .

Q: In fact, that's in the collection of stories, Criers and Kibitzers, Kibitzers and Criers, *that I wanted to ask you about first. In the introduction to that book, you mention that these early stories of yours are in the realist tradition, which you write, "presumes to deal . . . with cause and effect, with some deep need in readers—in all of us—for justice." Is the realist tradition where you advise young writers to begin?*

Yes. For *young* writers. Certainly we have the example of the story you heard today [in the undergraduate class]. That was hardly in the realistic tradition nor did I encourage her to write a story that was in the realistic tradition. Except when I made the suggestion that it really be about a bike trip. And were the story to have been about some eight-year-old on his bicycle striking out to the next neighborhood over, that *would* have been in the realistic tradition.

Q: And it might have worked better?

Of course it would. On the other hand, I don't really think that ultimately people should write about what they know—what's happened to them, their own experiences. Of course we all think our lives are important and dramatic even, but we make a mistake when we think that they're *shaped* and dramatic. The tendency when people are writing from experience is to put everything in: If it happened, it goes in. And as you know, writing is as much an act of criticism as anything else. You have to know what the hell doesn't go in.

I'll give you an example. When I was in the army from '55 to '57, we were invited to a bris [the Jewish ritual of circumcision]. A relative of mine had a daughter who had just given birth, and my wife, Joan, and myself and everyone else on the East Coast were invited to Washington—I was stationed in Virginia—where we were put up in hotels. Well, aside from my uniform, which I knew wasn't really what I should wear to this celebration, the only good clothes I had were a clean pair of pants and a shirt. So we went up for the weekend and were entertained at some grand hotel in Washington, and I put on my nice pants, except that there was a little L-shaped tear in the trousers, a tiny little thing. Joan had sewn it but you could still see the tear, the stitching, right on the knee—I think the right knee, since that's the knee I'm touching now and the body knows. And I sat down with some cousins, there are always cousins, and I—see, I'm putting everything in; I don't have enough sense to leave anything out. I'm telling you *my* story—but I'll go on.

We had gone to dinner [the night before the bris] at this major-league hotel and the younger people sat at this long, long table. Now all my other cousins, the guys and women who were not in the army, some of whom were married, all of them were doing brilliantly. They knew that I had aspirations to be a writer, since I publicly announced, "I'm a writer! I don't really belong in the army! I'm really a writer!" Well, I wasn't really a soldier, that part was true. And people were sort of patronizing me. Not putting me down, exactly, but patronizing me *and* putting me down. And so the next day at the bris, in my sewn pair of pants, I'm sitting next to my cousin, and she noticed my pants.

She said, "Stanley, don't you have the courtesy to wear an entire pair of pants, an unbroken, unseamed, unstitched pair of pants to my nephew's bris?" And I'd been boiling from the night before, and so I just got up in a fury and I said to Joan, "Come on, we're leaving, we're getting out of here. I don't want to stay with these people anymore! Blah blah blah!" And I walked into a closet. And when I got out of the closet, I said, "Where's the door," and I found the door, and I decided right there that I was going to avenge myself by writing a story called "Next Year in Jerusalem."

I tried to write that damn thing forever. I must have worked on that fucking story for three or four years. And it was no good. It was no good because it had *happened* to me, and I couldn't get enough distance from the damn thing. So, writing from experience is not charming to me. [Philip] Roth certainly writes what he knows, and he does it blessedly. But I don't advise young people to do it.

Q: One of the things I thought you were doing in the undergraduate class today was helping this young woman create the story that was absent. One of your students told me you were called "the story doctor."

It's apocryphal. But that *is* what I do. You see, particularly the young kids don't know where the story is, and I do try to help them find it. If they know that, if they can recognize where . . . I mean, she really did unconsciously write a story that was potentially a good story. But she didn't know where the good elements were. I am a tinkerer with other people's stuff.

Q: And the graduate class is another thing? It seemed to me a kind of master editorial class. At that level, I suppose, you can do line-by-line editing.

Right. It would be foolish to line edit in the undergraduate class. You'd drive yourself nuts. But some people even in the graduate class need help to find the story. For instance, Miss X is working on a novella that's going along just fine. But originally, last year, before she came to it, she was writing scenes that were fine but when you put them all together they didn't spell M-O-T-H-E-R. She was having trouble locating what she wanted to write about. On the other hand, Miss Y is a very mature writer and so when we discuss her stuff we go for the beauties. Since she doesn't always get everything right, we discuss the mistakes, too. Now, the young woman sitting to her right, Miss Z, is immensely talented. But she has a tendency to write from ideas, to begin with some kind of abstract idea she has of geography; but all you have to do is point this out to her and she knows. It varies from student to student. Today, Miss X's stuff is not necessarily the best, it's simply the most perfect. You know what I mean? It's very craftily done.

Q: Which brings me to the subject of style—first, your style.

You probably can't teach style.

Q: You write in the introduction to Criers and Kibitzers, *again, about. . .*

The revenge of style.

Q: Exactly. "Whatever spin," you write, "whatever 'English' [the writer] puts on the ball is his. It's his call. He leads, you follow. He leads, you play catch-up (It's the wallow in the ego again, the self's flashy mud-wrassle.)"

Well, the writers I admired, really admired, were Henry James, Melville—what the hell did I know, I hadn't read anyone else—William Faulkner, primarily Faulkner, and Norman Corwin, who was a radio writer during the forties. At the end of the war he wrote something called "A Note of Triumph," which was a celebration of V-E Day. It was produced by CBS. I was, what, fourteen years old when the War ended? And this program, which was probably prepared months in advance, was just thrilling to me. He had a phrase about God, "who furred the fox against the time of winter." And boy, my fourteen-year-old hackles rose up against the back of my neck. "Furred the fox against the time of winter."

I guess that was the first time I was conscious that you can say things in certain ways. Not just, "God made all creatures, big and little." But when I started to write I wasn't writing like that. It was only when I got through reading these people, and imitating Faulkner slavishly, and recognizing finally that I was imitating Faulkner slavishly, that I threw out the bad parts and worked on the good parts.

Q: And you mentioned that it took upheavals in your life as well.

Right. But I don't think just because someone is run over, say, that the light goes on and you write the "St. Louis Blues." But I'll tell you how many years it took. I was working on *George Mills* in 1976 when I was teaching at Boston University; I started it even earlier that year here in St. Louis but then took time off to write *The Living End*, which came out in '79. And when I finished *George Mills*—which was published in '82—I realized that I had found whatever my voice really is, though it exists in patches in *The Dick Gibson Show* and *A Bad Man*. But everything before those books I would repudiate. I mean, I don't *really* repudiate them.

Q: If it took so much time, then, what about students who rush it, who take on a style that isn't theirs? Gail Godwin said she used to tell her students never to impose a style. I would wonder, since your own style is individual and powerful, with your "delight in language as language," whether any of your students try to take it on?

Well, that *has* happened, but not with the graduate students. There used to be a 400-level undergraduate course I taught and there was a kid in it who gave me back myself, and I thought, "This is terrible, they ought to shoot this guy, or shoot me, one of the two."

For me, if I feel a riff going on, even if it'll stall the book, I'll probably use the riff and leave the book down the street someplace. But you have to learn the balance. There's a young man in the undergraduate course—the best writer there—he does riffs, he has a style. It gets in the way of what he's trying to say. He has more style than he knows what to do with, and he can't really pin it to a story. But if he finds the story to pin it to, he'll do something as a writer. Everybody has his own particular problems.

Of course, sometimes what helps is when I tell them to read so-and-so. I was talking about Miss Z before, who writes from ideas. When she told me some business about space and geography, I didn't know what the hell she meant. But what occurred to me as we were speaking was Faulkner's *Light in August*. Within the course of that book a lot of people are making trips, but they're not nostalgic about hometowns or the fact that they've been dislocated. These voyages Joe Christmas makes in his life are genuinely that, circular. So I told her to read *Light in August*, to help inform what she's doing. I meant to ask her today when I saw her what she made of it.

Q: Do you write just as well, by the way, during the academic year?

I do it comfortably now. Oh, I can't do it more than a page and a half at a time, and that's four hours' work, after which I find myself exhausted. I finished a book that's going to be coming out in March [1993, *Van Gogh's Room at Arles*] and I've been working on a short story, waiting for a novel to come. But I can't possibly get up the head of steam I need for a novel when I teach. So I diddle around on this short story until classes are over.

Q: I'd like to ask you about "moral" fiction. Your work has sometimes been called that, and Harold Brodkey has said, "Moral questions for [Elkin's characters] are not hovering and inexpressible— are not implied—but are present, expressible—and expressed." Other people have said similar things. If that has meaning at all to you, is it something you try to transmit to your students as well?

Well, what I would say is, the writer's obligation is to give every character the best lines. *Every* character. Now to the extent that he gives every character the best lines, he's a moral writer. Because a good line cannot happen without energy. A character might be saying devastating, awful things, but if he convinces you... did you ever read a book George Steiner wrote about Hitler, who's found in a South American jungle and brought back by Israeli commandos and is asked to explain himself? And Hitler doesn't do it, doesn't do it, doesn't do it. And then Steiner gives him an *incredible* speech. A marvelous speech. Which is totally antisemitic. It doesn't convince *me*, but it convinces me that Hitler is working from these premises.

Q: From the character.

Right. I don't think it was a successful book, but it sure as hell was a successful speech. And have you seen *Glengarry Glen Ross*, the motion picture? It's wonderful. It's a lesson in dialogue. And in plotting. But primarily in dialogue. People are not talking any poetry but the poetry of the streets. The poetry of door-to-door, actually, because they're all salesmen. It's just fantastic how good [David] Mamet's ear is. I mention it because these people don't have a moral bone in their body. But there's a long speech in the beginning given by a guy who sets goals for the salesmen, which if they don't meet they get canned, and he's just a vicious son of a bitch. Yet he talks and you're hypnotized. Everything he says is pure poetry. That, I would submit, has a kind of morality because it has a kind of integrity. It has a linguistic integrity which absolutely defines the character.

Q: Not "moral," you mean, in the sense of a Judeo-Christian ethic.

Right. Except it *is* a kind of sermon.

Q: That must be an extremely difficult thing to get young writers to do.

Mamet is in his fifties. But young writers have to understand that this is what they should aim for. But I was going to make a point earlier on. I told you I really don't like teaching undergraduates writing, because these kids are too young; they don't *know* themselves. They may be well read—and those that *are* are better writers—but they haven't been around the block. Moral dialogue would sound phony coming out of a mouth that is not attached to human beings in a situation. So what I do with the undergraduates—and if I can get them to do this I feel I've done my job—I teach from situation. I try to get them to understand what the hell a situation is.

As a matter of fact the first day of class, always, I tell them the story of Bartleby the Scrivener, which I think is a marvelous story, and is a marvelous story because of the tightness of the situation. And the only thing that can happen in that story is what happens in that story, because of the tightness of the situation. I hope I demonstrate this, and then I ask them to jot down a situation in seven minutes. They turn them in and invariably they're bad. But I can point out *why* they're bad and how they could be made good. If we change term A and make it term B, B to C. It's toward that end that I direct every class. I am, or try to be, a story doctor, if the story is sick. And you can tell that some students know themselves because today they picked up on why the story you heard wasn't good. I didn't have to say a word.

Q: John Gardner, for one, wrote that "art instructs."

Was that in *On Moral Fiction*?

Q: Yes.

Well, that ain't what art does. Art makes things. Did you ever see *Sunday in the Park with George*? There's a marvelous song that Sondheim does where Serat's mistress says, "George, it's so hot, it's so hot. I wish I had a hat or something." And so he has this song to sing. "Dot dot dot, pling pling pling"—all these sounds and words, you don't quite know what they are—then he says, "A hat, a hat, I made a hat, where there never was a hat." That's what art is. You make a hat where there never was a hat. That's the pleasure, it seems to me, of writing.

Reading is a different pleasure. Reading takes you away from everything. You forget what the time is, you forgot you have to pee—well, maybe you don't forget *that*—but the reader concentrates, while the writer concentrates on making something. I could never go to a political conference. I vote for the right guy. I want the right people to lose the right war, and I give to the United Way, but I don't regard myself as a political person. They're wearing these buttons now at this conference. It says, "I am Salman Rushdie." I would never wear that button. Some people feel quite comfortable doing it; I don't.

Q: So art doesn't instruct at all?

Well, it does a little. It ultimately teaches you taste. Taste in fiction, taste in poetry, taste in music, taste in life. But I was up at Bread Loaf the summer that Gardner died. In fact he died not long afterward, perhaps a month after I saw him. And that summer he came and announced to the world, "I was wrong about moral fiction. It's not moral; political is where it's at. Political." But when he says that writing is morality, then it's politics, he's wrong in both instances. Poor John. And I say "poor John" with great affection, because he's not around to defend himself.

Q: But he had a powerful way of writing about writing.

As if from Mount Olympus. I wrote an essay in a book called *Pieces of Soap* about overrated masterpieces, and the first sentence in that essay, and I believe it, is, "There is nothing so convincing as an opinion." If somebody says, "Cripples should not be permitted on the street after dark," somebody will think, "Well, maybe that's a good idea." It's a stupid example, but I remember when I was with Random House and Joe Fox was my editor—he was a wonderful editor, the one editor I had who took me to the better restaurants all the time!—and Sinatra had been in New York singing and Fox had been there and met Sinatra afterwards. Joe had brown socks on, and Sinatra said something like, "Eh, this guy has brown socks on. What kind of a guy wears brown socks?" Fox was humiliated and thought, "Yeah, what kind of guy *does* wear brown socks?" Because there is nothing so convincing as an opinion.

Q: I have to ask you finally about creating illusion. In your last novel, The MacGuffin, *you draw a distinction between the plots, plans, and intrigues of life, and the banality of it. Your character Bobbo Druff, City Commissioner of Streets, he's an ordinary guy. But he speaks of the "spirit of narrative in his life, his sense of closure. . . ."*

That's what a MacGuffin is. Look, Druff lives in two different worlds. He lives in the world where he goes to dances with his wife when he first meets her, just another undergraduate student getting necking time in, the ordinary. And in that same scene he lives in a world where she wants to live in a boarding house—now this is *not* the ordinary. Later on he lives in the ordinary world where his wife's hearing aid fails and he goes out to buy the batteries, but at the same time he's getting the batteries he's using them as a cover to buy a prophylactic to run around on his wife.

By the same token, what creates interest in fiction, it seems to me, is the jarring of juxtaposition. In the wonderful television series "Upstairs Downstairs" we had the ordinary life of the domestics and the ordinary life of the powerful people who lived upstairs, and the magic happened when the two got together. I think you have to have "the strange displacements of the ordinary." It's a phrase I use in *The Dick Gibson Show*. That makes for fiction.

Q: And if one were trying to convey "reality," which, then, is the more real: that intrigue, that MacGuffin—or just the banal "housekeeping of existence" that Druff contends with?

It depends on whose reality you're portraying, of course. But if you were portraying *my* reality, I mean just my life as a cripple, I mean it would be so boring that you wouldn't read past page five. One of the novellas I just finished, called *Her Sense of Timing* [in *Van Gogh's Room at Arles*], does in fact portray my life as a cripple, except that it's my life as a cripple under extraordinary circumstances. I'm just as crippled as I am now—almost as crippled, pretty crippled, this character has many "deficits," the way doctors describe this thing. But in the very first scene when his wife is holding suitcases in her hands, he says, "Where are you going?" and she says, "Goodbye, I'm leaving you, the marriage is over." He says, "How can you leave me now?" She says, "I'm tired of being your wife. It's too much hard work. I'm leaving. The cab is waiting downstairs." He says, "But tomorrow's the party for the students." And she leaves and he's committed to giving this party alone. I mean, the ordinary life he leads as a cripple is easy when he has somebody there to help him. It almost kills him when he's alone. That makes for a fiction.

Q: You write of Druff, "It wasn't just buying batteries for your wife's hearing aid. It was this. Mostly it was this. The deep, hidden peristaltics of mood. . . . Life goes on. . . ."

Druff *c'est moi.* I mean, I'm sixty-two, in the book he's pushing sixty. When you get to be my age you need a MacGuffin—when you get to our age, Druff's and mine.

George Garrett

(PHOTOGRAPH BY SUSAN GARRETT)

George Garrett was born in Orlando, Florida, in 1929. Receiving his undergraduate and graduate degrees from Princeton University, he has been and continues to be a guiding force in the development of writing programs in this country. He has taught at Bennington College, the University of Michigan, Wesleyan University, Rice University, the University of South Carolina, Hollins College, and the University of Virginia, among other places; he has been director of several programs, been president of the Associated Writing Programs (AWP), written essays on teaching manifestly broad in perspective, and—as "a real measure," says Nicholas Delbanco—"probably has . . . more books dedicated to him [by former students] than any other American author."

George Garrett speaks here about the history of writing programs, his own open and inclusive teaching philosophy, and the intersection of teaching and writing. "If I were going to teach," Garrett says in the prologue to a recent collection of essays, *The Sorrows of Fat City* (1992), "if I were teaching to earn my keep, then I would surely need to know as much as I could, from practice and experience, about many different kinds of writing."

These "different kinds of writing" span seven novels, seven volumes of poetry, six books of short fiction, dozens of essays and reviews, several screenplays, and a literary biography (*James Jones*, 1984)—in sum, "as large and significant a body of work as any writer of his generation," writes R.H.W. Dillard. His novels include the celebrated "Elizabethan" trilogy: *Death of the Fox* (1971), *The Succession* (1983), and *Entered from the Sun* (1990). He is the editor, also, of eighteen books.

Winner of the T. S. Eliot Award in 1989 and the PEN/Malamud Award in 1990, George Garrett's newest novel is *The King of Babylon Shall Not Come Against You*. He is currently Hoyns Professor of English at the University of Virginia, which is where this conversation took place, after one of his advanced graduate workshops.

The University of Virginia, in Charlottesville, offers a B.A. in English and a two-year M.F.A. in Creative Writing.

Q: In an essay you wrote in 1970, about your role as teacher, you said, "I consider . . . myself a participant rather than an observer, learning myself as we go along together." And then, "I play by ear and I improvise as I go along." It sounds as though you were speaking about teaching writing as a creative process itself, as more an art than a craft?

Maybe as a *performance* art in a curious way. It certainly burns up some of the same energies, with instant gratification or disaster. Of course, the disadvantage of just "winging it" like I do, improvising, participating as just another member of the workshop, is that you have more mediocre or run-of-the-mill classes than you might if you were highly organized and systematic. But every once in a while you have an extremely successful session, and that's so heady you want to do it all again.

There's something else, too. Maybe I'm justifying [my way] a little, but even a run-of-the-mill class or workshop is not really doing anybody any harm. At the very best, students get to write and get some response; it may not be what they're always looking for or what they need, even, but it's usually not frustrating or negative for them.

Q: Whereas a more rigid system might be negative?

Well, the more rigid systems, and there are a lot of them, tend to be rather rigid critically. The students fall into the system and then they have to unlearn it when they get around other people; they become sort of nasty negative critics of everything, demanding more of their peers than they ought to.

Q: There did seem to be a rather high level of support in your class last night.

Yeah, they really want to do that; they've sort of figured it out early on. Sometimes I have to tell them they *have* to say something overtly in that way, that I hope everyone is supportive of the goals of the writer even if you disapprove of them. And it's always possible to have one person—it's like group therapy in that way—who is extremely opinionated and negative and causes a lot of people grief. We'll see how this class goes; it's still at the level of getting to know each other. It may yet lead to some arguments down the line. I hope it does.

Q: In answer to the question "Can writing be taught?" you've said that people can always be taught "to write as they do, if it's worth the effort." Since you've taught undergrads and graduates, even setting up writing programs elsewhere, I'd be curious to know if you thought it was *always worth the effort.*

Well, at the undergraduate level first, maybe the perception's changed rather than the fact of it, but the writing class has become one of the very few opportunities on the college level to have a close rhetorical study of manuscript.

In 1970, say, nobody was taking on or reviewing the people who didn't know how to read or write. We're performing that function in a very effective way now. It's partly a factor of the economy that some of these undergraduates are in school rather than out doing something else—there aren't any jobs, after all. But they're *not* wasting time; they're doing reading and writing and some of them *will* be writers, probably without any correlation to talent. In fact, judging from the past, probably some of the less talented ones will have considerable success, and some of the really bright ones will move on to something else, go to law school. And that's fine. It goes back to what we were saying about not doing any harm.

And look at the old way. When I first went to college in 1947 there were only about two places that had creative writing courses. In the early days a place like Virginia had a wonderful old man named John Coleman who taught a course called "Advanced Composition: Studies in Narrative Technique." *If* you got in there, you discovered that you in fact wrote short stories. Other schools had their own people. Rice had George Williams;

Duke had William Blackburn. Most of these people taught maybe one course and if people wanted to get in, it was hard. Coleman and the others seriously felt that a considerable amount of their function was to *discourage* people from a career in writing, to be very demanding at that level for those who didn't show quite a bit of polish and tenacity and experience and talent, to treat them harshly enough so that they would get the hell out. They felt that they were gatekeepers. They were gate-keepers to their courses and, in a way, to writing.

Q: When did the change occur, historically, from this more exclusionary group to today's relative openness?

Middle to the second half of the 1950s. It caught on like a lot of academic fashions and was really a response to a demand from an older student body that wasn't around when it was fulfilled. We had lots of thirty-year-old people after World War II on the G.I. Bill who were much more demanding and really pushed for courses. When I first started college, there were no courses at Princeton University for books written after 1900. We argued and fussed and they finally put in a course in the summer and then again during the year—*one* course. Now everybody has dozens of courses in all manner of modern and contemporary literature. That's a radical change and along with it—both things influencing each other—came the creative writing courses and the hiring of writers to be part of the academic community, which is an interesting phenomenon, too.

The old-timers who taught in the late thirties, maybe they were writers themselves and maybe not. As late as 1955 Robert Frost was probably one of only five poets hired by an institution. I remember when Wesleyan hired Richard Wilbur in 1956, it was still considered quite a bold stroke then, an adventurous thing to hire a poet to be on your faculty. Now everybody has one. And the courses create their own demand. As soon as you have one course, you have people who want to take it again, and soon the curriculum becomes more and more expansive.

So the old teachers in writing were a bit like football coaches today who recruit on the basis of established ability, not on potential. In football today, they really don't have time to fool with creating players. Today, nobody goes up to a head coach and says, "I would like to learn to kick." I mean, forget it, no one has time. The old-time writing teachers were like the modern-day football coaches, they didn't have time. "If you can write," they said, "we will read it and pass it on to the *New Yorker*." It's fundamentally in conflict with today's notion that it's the students who make the choice of wishing to study writing. And the fact that a significant number of them who try don't achieve anything as writers is not in my view a harmful thing. They're learning a discipline that has many values.

Look, every day I see walking up this street, up the hill, in time for the school bus, kids from the local junior high school. For some reason everybody in Charlottesville has to have a musical instrument; they all study as part of their public schooling. So you see trombones and cornets and violins. Probably *nobody*, despite all the effort that's being spent, not one person is going to be a violinist at Carnegie Hall or play with a major band. But in music nobody worries about it. No one sees it as waste. In writing, it ought to be the same. A lot of them are not going to do it. As long as you make it very clear that it's difficult, that this is a thing to learn, I think it should be encouraged. Discouragement is going to happen anyway, much more than the old-timers realized, I think.

Q: Madison Bell told me he wondered why so few students at Iowa go on to publish manuscripts when all of them are so talented.

I noticed something else, too, at Iowa. Years ago, when Paul Engle retired, I was one of the people they considered to run that workshop. I went out there and studied it pretty closely and the first thing I noticed was that it was huge, about 150 people in the program, but only about ten of them were visible. Everywhere you went, reading, lectures, there were the same ten or twelve people, established as their leading lights. The other 138 were down in the bowels of the library somewhere grading compositions. This is a factor that has only really recently come to the fore.

Q: Is this related to the question you've raised about the degree to which writers should engage in academic study versus actual writing?

Well, I was brought out to Michigan to start the writing program there. They already had some writing courses, they had the Hopwood Lectures, but basically anything I wanted to do, I could. And I made one fatal mistake. The director of graduate studies said very casually, "Would you like to have a language requirement?" And I thought, "Why not? Sure." This has become a horrible obstacle. You have to be really good to pass. It got me to thinking about the burden of academics.

From Michigan I came here, and here the only requirement for the graduate writers is a workshop and one academic course per term. *One* per term. Many other schools require two at least, because the idea of the writing program at almost every other school in the country is to fill up graduate classes, to get enough bodies to maintain, say, a Spenser course, which you wouldn't ordinarily be able to do because not enough people signed up. Here they have the largest straight graduate English program in the country, so they don't need us. In fact, they had to make room for us.

There are other schools, though, that do interesting things in this way. The University of Arkansas [Fayetteville] is the toughest creating writing program in the country. Theoretically you should be able to get your M.F.A. from them in three years, but nobody ever has; it takes four or five with a tremendous amount of course work. It was founded by all these people we'll be seeing a lot of under the Clinton Administration—Miller Williams, who writes speeches, and James Whitehead. They were defectors from Iowa, which had gotten too big, and they were like Luther, getting back to the original Church. So they created this small program at Arkansas and made entrance requirements extremely demanding on M.F.A. students—much higher GREs, better grades—and then they make you work twice as hard once you're in. It's killing. But out of it comes wild rebels like Barry Hannah.

Similarly at the University of North Carolina, Greensboro, which has the only graduate writing program in the state, they are a much superior lot. In regular graduate programs in the state, at Chapel Hill or Duke or N.C. State, it's uneven. But at Greensboro, where it's only writers, the students are quite outstanding and from all over the country.

Q: You've written, "It's not necessarily the chief purpose and function of a writing course to produce writers." What is the goal, then?

To put it much more simply, it's to satisfy a felt need by these people. They select the route they're going—it's true, without knowing what they're getting into, any more than anybody else—but in part we're just fulfilling a stated need.

Q: "They need," you've written, "to practice the five senses, the feeling, the imagination. . . . Thus writing, whether or not it results in the encouragement of one real or true writer, is a vital part of education." In that sense, the writing class might do things academic classes can't.

That's true. And I think it's had an effect on composition classes, making them more open to imaginative writing.

Of course, a key person in all of this was [R. V.] Cassill. He was invited back to the Associated Writing Programs in Boston, which he founded, and shocked them all by saying that it's been quite fun and wonderful, but for the sake of American literature you writers should all get out of academics and go to work. No one has gotten over the shock. But the strangest kind of confirmation he got was from scientists, who talked to him at Brown. They said, "We need institutions for the lab equipment, but the association between science and the academy has not been entirely beneficial." Cassill feels this way about writing.

Plus, the other major argument you're hearing a lot of lately—particularly among older writers, the whole loop of people who go to college, then to a graduate writing program, then publish several stories, then end up teaching writing—is that in some ways it's not beneficial in the universities. That's the kind of John Aldridge pitch.

Q: And where do you come out on that?

A kind of large shrug. In some cases it's not beneficial and in some it is. I don't think you can generalize. I see the down-side arguments about creative writing programs, but they've been there all along—and so what? There *is* a danger that with over-organization writers can be seen as a club. And maybe this has happened to a degree in poetry. A lot of poets that I like seem to be outside the loop and I'm stunned that they never get any attention. The same old names keep cropping up. And maybe it's getting a little that way in fiction, but I don't think so. It's so broad.

Q: John Aldridge, in the interview you did with him, said, "Writing programs on the whole seem to me to be turning out literary carpenters and construction engineers, but they cannot create talent."

But nobody ever said they could! John is a little older than I am, the older generation. He came into academe as a critic, he's a trailblazer, and he has kept it up. His most recent books are about the most recent writers, which opened up the doors to a lot of criticism. But he still has the mindset of the gatekeeper, that theoretically we should be scouring the country looking for potential geniuses and then helping them. That would be ideal except that's not what anyone is going to do. It's true, we may be missing them completely. But maybe the people who do not get into the system of creative writing are going to do fine anyway because they have something to rebel against and be contemptuous of, which is always helpful in a writer's career. And the people in the program, some of them are going to awake and sing and some are going to go to sleep. That's true of law school and medical school. I'm sure there are some people who could have been brain surgeons who rather decide to be dermatologists because it's nine-to-five.

Q: So the argument that writing programs hone too-slick writers, as if in an assembly line . . . ?

Well, I guess a part of what he's saying is that the writers they produce are technically skilled but lack heart in the way other generations didn't. But I'm not sure that the technical skill is all that high to begin with. They've learned enough technique in order to get started. What we have to do is see that young writers don't develop too many habits too early.

There is a parallel to this in movie writing. A very good lesson I learned when I went out there was from a cameraman. We got talking and I was very impressed by all the good things he could do with the camera. But he said, "Don't get too interested in this. This is mechanics, man. I do this for a living and I'm good at it and I understand it as a machine, but," he went on, "I only have to use this stuff if the script is nothing. You write me a good-enough script and I'll turn the camera on automatic and go take a coffee break. If your end of it is good enough, no one cares about technique at all. Technique is there to save material that otherwise doesn't get across."

Now that's slightly exaggerated but not too much. Writers love to go out there and think of shots and angles, but what you really want is character and story.

Q: Do you have to keep working with students, then, to prevent them from overrefining?

Well, in writing, if something works there's a great inclination to do it again. It's no fun to be thrashing about. Yet the whole process of developing as a writer *is* experimentation. We were talking with David Huddle two or three days ago, and I was pleased he agreed with me that all that we learn in writing a book, at the end of it, is how we should have done it in the first place. And that's of no particular carryover value to the next one unless we want to write exactly the same book, which very few people want to do except in the world of extreme commercial success and formula, cranking it out.

Q: Van Gogh, paint me another sunflower.

Yeah, and it seems to me there's one other aspect to this that we're not talking about, and that's that writers already have certain habits and obsessions and inhibitions that they're not going to get around, even beginners. They certainly shouldn't be encouraged to put the wagons in the circle and defend their own limitations to the death. Writing classes may be the last chance to open up and try everything. Adulthood is not going to give you much opportunity to do that.

Q: Grace Paley has said she wanted to stay as open and ignorant in the art of teaching as she wants them to remain in the art of writing.

She's quite right about that. I never had a creative course, but I've been sitting in them for more years than I want to count. And there are always some students you don't reach, and always a minority you do. Which is another reason why it's a good idea to have enough teachers around some sort of little program, because that way students can shop around and find somebody with whom they feel at ease. Some of these kids urgently want somebody who's got a completely different style from one like mine; they want a structured class, and they respond very well to that. Those kids would go crazy in my classes, and vice versa. Personality enters into it to an extent. So if they have other doors and other rooms, then it's possibly not very harmful. They're going to find the same thing with editors if they go on to become writers: There are some they will work better with than others. And this changes all the time as *you* change.

Q: Which goes back to what you were saying about writers doing the same thing again and again. Perhaps it's not exactly a narrowing. . .

But it's not an expanding, either.

Q: In that sense, do you keep the marketplace, which from a commercial viewpoint can implicitly or even explicitly ask for a certain product, away from students?

Here's where I part company from some of my colleagues: I try to keep students aware, in various indirect ways so that it doesn't impose on their work, of what's happening in the publishing scene. They're already interested and they haunt the bookstores. They're special for that reason.

Secondly, my rule is: I don't encourage them. I seldom say, "Why don't you send this out for publication?" If they come to me and say, "Can I do it?" then I'm glad to help them as much as I can in the details of it, I'm prepared to be practical when they ask for it or when they're ready for it, but I won't push them.

And if there's somebody in here, which there often is, writing something for which there is absolutely no market but that generates a high level of interest or entertainment—such as a student some years ago at Wesleyan [who] only wrote variations on "The Untouchables" gangster stories set in Chicago, which were really fun in class but nobody was going to touch them— they should not be deprived of the opportunity. People should be able to write with absolute disregard of the marketplace if they want. To those with their eyes cocked to the idea of getting something published, the main thing you have to tell them is to relax a little and get their work done.

Q: Would it help if students weren't so young when they started learning to write?

Probably, if I were the Ayatollah, I would have a break take place between being an undergraduate and coming into a program. I try to compensate. I remember a sculptor at Princeton saying that all Princeton graduates should be required to take one year off and sell shoes, every damn one of them. Bennington of course has their term off every year and the kids always end up in Acapulco doing a survey of beaches! But anyway, he did have an idea, and it's not bad. For most of this century, up until very recently, we did the same thing they still do in France, like universal military training: You had to go off and do two years of service, and in the course of that you met people from all walks of life. So it was never a problem for those generations to relate to other folks because they had *lived* with them.

In the absence of that system, we handle the graduate admissions differently. We get two hundred applications a year for the program and we do it initially entirely on the basis of the manuscript. That's all we see and we eliminate people unanimously. When we're down to ten percent, into the second level, at that point we look to other factors. And one of the other factors is whether somebody has been out doing something else for a while, which is a plus. We've ended up with lawyers, nonfiction writers. And the age difference is a benefit to everyone. They have a different kind of shit detector. They *will* speak up:

"It doesn't work that way." And it does keep kids from writing clichéd stories about their parents, for instance, with people their parents' age in the same room.

Q: So to have a break early might be good, but, as you say, for every rule you can find fifty exceptions. How many writers, for instance, wrote their best book in their twenties?

That's right. In other words, if you send them off to Alaska during their most productive years, they may come back and do nothing.

Q: And it may be too much to ask of any program, much less teachers, to be able to predict which way it will go.

So far, they've spent millions and millions of dollars in my lifetime trying to study ways to define and correlate creativity with actual performance, and they've never been able to do much. Saul Bellow said a researcher once paid him ten thousand dollars to come take some psychological tests in Berkeley—they had Capote there, too—and what they ended up with was the feeling that writers had more willpower. Willpower is a nice nineteenth-century term. And if *that's* all, it doesn't tell you anything, except maybe that discipline helps.

Q: I'd like to ask you for a moment about the University of Virginia being in the South. Is there a regional value to any program insofar as it affects the training that writers get while they're there?

That's a hard question to answer, but on the other hand there are some patterns. Under law, we must take, in the university as a whole, fifty percent of the students from Virginia in order to get state funding. It *is* a state university. But in the writing program a great many of them tend to be from out of state even though there is a very high out-of-state tuition.

But in the large sense, some of the best creative writing programs are in institutions in the South: Hollins, Greensboro,

Tuscaloosa, Arkansas, Alabama, the University of Florida, and especially Florida International University in North Miami, which has a very young and lively faculty. I think one of the reasons writing programs caught on and got rooted here was that many of the regular programs in Southern universities were not all that good. This was an opportunity for visibility and for excellence at the easiest and cheapest way you could possibly imagine. You don't have to build a huge lab; you just hire some writers and start a writing program. So Southern universities became hospitable because they saw it as an opportunity to make a name for themselves when they had none.

Plus, the South accepted the career of writing as one that is as useful as any other. There's one reasonable peculiarity about life in the South that's never spoken about, and that is: With the single exception of Thomas Wolfe, you don't have *any* Southern writers writing books about how *hard* it was growing up to be a writer. We've practically escaped that genre, which is uniform throughout the world. There are lots of reasons why that's true, but mainly I think it's because it's been such a poverty-ridden region that, as my grandfather said, writing is as good a way to be poor as any other. It beats being poor and digging in the hot sun!

So economically and socially, writing was hospitable here, and in terms of the institutions it was a quick fix—even though a significant number of the kids are from the West, the North, and the Middle West. You can go a long way around here before you'll hear a Southern accent.

Q: So it's not as if you have a petri dish of pure "Southern" experience.

John Casey is fiction writer and teacher here; he's from Boston and Rhode Island; Charles Wright is a poet from Tennessee, but Gregory Orr is from Michigan. The mix is true all through the Southern schools. Barthelme is running the Hattiesburg [Mississippi] one. So it isn't an encouragement of regionalism, though it may be true that having creative writing programs has meant more to Southern schools than maybe it has elsewhere.

Q: Your 1970 essay, the one I asked you about earlier, appeared in a book called Writers as Teachers/Teachers as Writers *[edited by Jonathan Baumbach]. You've been both writer and teacher for so long, with such effect, I'd be curious to know what influence, if any,* teaching *writing can have on writing proper.*

Provided it doesn't become obsessive, working with manuscripts can be helpful to a writer. On the other hand, I really do prefer not to teach more than one workshop a semester. I'm teaching two this fall and I really prefer one workshop and one literature course. It works better for both. Next semester I'm teaching "The Image of Hollywood in Novels and Films," and I did "Shakespeare in the Movies" and "The Literature of War." That's a benefit.

But the life of the writer in the academy has other consequences. I could see it coming. Lots of people today in America write in fragmentary forms, short forms, linked stories, and a lot of it has to do with how much time we have to work. Much of what's produced by people working in institutions probably does lack, for better or worse, the precise qualities of sustained fiction. It would be very hard for Tolstoy to write any of his novels while trying to teach a creative writing course. People who are not academics have moved in this direction also; Kurt Vonnegut, though he has been in academics, basically does his books in fragments, always has.

But one should also talk about the simple business of making a living. Remember, I backed up into this by need; I was already an English teacher and they needed somebody to teach writing courses. Until very recently, however, it wasn't possible for someone to earn a living essentially as a writer but not necessarily off their writing. *Teaching* writing has made it possible. For example, David Huddle said that the most money he'd ever gotten for anything he had written was four thousand dollars. And he's been a steady, productive, good writer. It would not have been possible a generation ago for a man to live like that. It was not possible for Faulkner, Fitzgerald, Hemingway to work in colleges—it wasn't an option. It was for Frost only, and that for only part of the time. They worked for movies, some of them, and it was possible to live on less, too, in those days, or of course to marry well!

So the opposite of the theory that the universities are supporting mediocrity is that a whole lot of writers who would never have had the chance now have an opportunity to contribute something to the national treasury. And this would not have been possible had not the universities opened their doors to writers. Universities are buying the time for these writers, and not paying very much for it.

There may be dangers. Writers may get the job on the basis of false elements like good reviews or visibility. There's a risk of corruption in academe. But this is a radical change unlike anything since the Middle Ages, when most writers were in monasteries. That was the institution that absorbed them. After that you had patronage. We have a tremendous number of writers— and so what if there may not be figures that stand out gigantically against the landscape? The landscape has *changed*. There are a tremendous number of more than competent, very good writers doing wonderful work, and you cannot believe this is a bad thing for the American scene. And it is also because of the university that so many up-until-now unrepresented ethnic minorities have found a home. As long as there is a literary scene in which people are encouraged, the richness and diversity in American literary culture is quite wonderful.

Q: The trade-off is not unfavorable, as you see it.

For the country at large, not at all. You can say, "There's a lot of mediocre stuff." But I think there's a great deal of very good stuff, too, and it's coming from all sorts of points that were not on the map before, all sorts of people who would never have had an opportunity to be a writer. There can be no harm in it. And the students get benefits, too. Unlike [in] the thirties and forties, income is not one of the requirements for admission. I think it's kind of wonderful to be in a class like this.

Gail Godwin

Gail Godwin was born in Birmingham, Alabama, in 1937 and raised in Asheville, North Carolina. She was a journalist for the *Miami Herald*, a U.S. Travel Service employee at the American Embassy in London, and an editorial assistant at the *Saturday Evening Post*, all before joining the Iowa Writers' Workshop, where she received her doctorate in English.

Since *The Perfectionists* (1970), Godwin has written two collections of stories and seven more novels, all widely read, among them *The Odd Woman* (1974), a National Book Award nominee, *Violet Clay* (1978) and *A Mother and Two Daughters* (1982), both American Book Award nominees, and the acclaimed *A Southern Family* (1987). Although she no longer teaches formally, her insight into the process of learning and the shape of a writing life becomes immediately evident in essays such as "Becoming a Writer" and "A Diarist on Diarists." She speaks here of the need for writers to develop "a capacity for associations," and indeed, in conversation at her home in Woodstock, New York, she dipped freely into pages of notes, pages of a work-in-progress, leather-bound diaries, and books on a shelf—all used knowingly as resources for the imagination.

"I would try to cultivate a mind-set in the young person," she says, "and the mind-set would be very simple: Paying attention, paying attention to what you are doing, knowing the names for things, knowing the names of weeds ... getting everything you can out of everything you know. Stories come out of this, plots come out of this, you get to know people better, simply by paying attention to what's before your eyes."

Gail Godwin has taught at the University of Iowa Writers' Workshop, Vassar College, and Columbia University. Her latest novel is *The Good Husband*.

The University of Iowa, in Iowa City, offers a B.A. in English and, in the graduate program known as the Iowa Writers' Workshop, a two-year M.F.A. in Creative Writing.

Q: You say you just found some notes from your days teaching?

Yes, here's one. [Reads.]

"If there's a choice between cleverness and compassion, choose compassion. If there's a choice between style and content, choose content. If you've got the right content, the style comes out of it."

Because you should never try to impose a style. Here's another: "Don't be afraid of being simple. Identify characters through dialogue and make it clear who is saying what. And dialect: a little bit goes a long way." (Old Joseph in *Wuthering Heights*, remember how he goes on and on and you just wish he'd go on a little less. A little dialect is fine because it gives you the language of the people, but then, well...) "A great writer must make the big connections. Character: be on everyone's side." That's a good one, too.

Q: It's strange you mention "connections," because that's a word that comes up quite a bit concerning your work and I want to ask you about it later. First, though, I read somewhere that you always wanted to write. Nevertheless, you started as a journalist in Miami, you worked in England. You found your way to writing only slowly. Today, the advice might be "go into a writing program." I'd be curious to know what you think now about the path you took.

I think if I had it to do over again, I'd do what I did: to live first and do many things and see many things, because otherwise writing becomes a career, and sometimes I'm appalled now talking to young writers interested in a career track. "How do I get an agent?" they say, not "How do I represent point of view?" They ask: "Who are the right people to know; what is the typical pattern for someone who is going to be a success; do you write a novel first or do you do stories?" Well, those are the wrong questions. Whereas I always wanted to write and I was writing—not very well—but living, too, and the interaction of both improves the material.

Q: Would you actually advise would-be writers to delay entry into a writing program?

I can't advise anyone, but I think if they're in a hurry, there are ways to do several things at once. You could travel, take courses. When I was in London and working for the travel service, I was always writing something. And at one point I did go and take an evening course for adults called "Fiction Writing." (I don't think the English go in for "Creative Writing.") It was at the City Literary Institute, which was this big, old, prisonlike building, and out of that came the first story I wrote that got published.

My teacher gave us an assignment; she wanted us to write a story about someone unlike ourselves. "If you were a woman be a man, be different, and imagine that person's life." And it's a good example of teaching that helped me draw on my life as I was living it and as I have lived it. You know, sometimes it takes years to build up. Another thing she did—she was an awfully good teacher; she worked for the BBC during the day and had a wonderful reading voice—she would just say, "I am going to read you an excellent story and we'll see why it's excellent," and she would read a story by Chekhov, and once she read a story by Muriel Spark. Then we'd talk about the techniques that made it so good.

Q: How in the world did you end up at Iowa, at the Writers' Workshop?

Well, I came back to New York City after working in England for five years and had a job fact checking at the *Saturday Evening Post.* I was quite desperate. And then an aunt died and left me five thousand dollars, which doesn't sound like anything now but it was just the perfect sum to get me out of there, and I knew just what I wanted to do: I wanted to go to the Iowa Writers' Workshop.

Q: It's just the sum that Margaret Gower [the protagonist in her 1991 novel, Father Melancholy's Daughter*] gets from the church collection to help her leave.*

How funny. You know I hadn't made that connection. That's why people probably do well with their analysts. *Of course*, it was just enough to get me out, so I got out and went to Iowa, and the story I used to get me in was the story of a priest that I had written in the workshop in England. They accepted me on the basis of that.

Q: Were you greatly influenced by anyone in particular at Iowa?

My teachers there that first year—that was such a wonderful year—were Kurt Vonnegut and José Donoso. Very different writers. José taught a course in the apprentice novel: Robert Musil's *Young Torless*, Thomas Wolfe's *Look Homeward, Angel*, D. H. Lawrence's *Sons and Lovers*. He had about a dozen apprentice novels about young people becoming artists. So you can imagine what a course *that* was for me. And then Kurt, he had that laid-back guru persona and he conveyed that if you pleased yourself, you'd please him. He was never cruel. He encouraged you to talk, and he listened. Kurt had sweetness. You felt when you were in the room with him that you had the potential to be likable. One lovely maxim he had was, "Being a good fiction writer is nothing more than being a good date." He was the one who read the story that I had written, which later became my first novel, *The Perfectionists*, and he'd put things in very light pencil on the side: "Wow," "First rate," and then at one point he put, "Sandbagging flashback," which means "That's too much for the reader." And he encouraged me. After I said I'll make this into a novel, he said, "It's very nice as a story." Then when I made it into a novel he said, "It's very nice as a novel."

Q: John Irving mentioned Vonnegut as well, his noninterventionist style of teaching.

Yeah, he wasn't a hands-on man at all.

Q: But it worked.

That worked, yes. And then the next year I had Robert Coover, who was stimulating in a different way. He was such a little magician; he would come to class with these ideas and force you to do them. For instance, he passed out examination blue books and gave us a scenario: "Someone finds a fragment of a misplaced story that Scheherazade told." So I wrote a story about a monk in the monastery in 1200, and he was cold and his fingers were cold and then he started writing about this fragment that they had found, and so in my case the story turned out really to be about the monk and the little things he drew in the margins and how cold he was and how he wished he could pray better. Everyone did their own thing. See, Coover had this vast energy, and then he took all the blue books home and, without a computer, typed them all up and collated them and mimeographed them—and then he had a critic from the English department, Robert Scholes, come and comment on our fragments. Coover was very interested in literary theory and ways of writing.

But the other thing I liked about my two years at Iowa was the other students who happened to be there. John Irving was there. I didn't know him very well but I went to his twenty-fourth birthday party. He lived in a tiny apartment and he made a writing room for himself in the closet. He fitted out that room with little stimulants to himself, things to egg him on: I can do it, I can do it. And John Casey was one of my friends and Jane Barnes, they were engaged then, and we talked writing all the time. I was very envious of Jane because she had a series of first-rate rejections from the *New Yorker*, and we'd read them over and say, "Oh, this is good." I was four years older than most of them, twenty-nine at the time, but no one had come right out of college, we'd all done other things, gone other places. And we were captivated by the craft of writing and fascinated by all the ways people had done it. We were always reading things, figuring out how Chekhov had written this sex scene without any nuts and bolts in it, and yet it's so wonderful—the one called "The Lady with the Dog." It's the way people really are when they're having an affair; it's those two people and their reactions. That's the kind of things we talked about. How it's done.

Q: And you stayed.

I stayed and got a master's in English, because I just kept taking English courses so I could read, and then I got a Ph.D. in English. My field was nineteenth-century British literature and my two specialties were modern allegory and visionary studies. Kafka, Blake, and Dostoevsky. And they allowed me to use the novel I published as a dissertation. So I ended up staying for four years and then went away for a year and did postdoctoral work at the University of Illinois. Then I was invited back to Iowa to teach in the writing program.

Q: Since you're speaking about literature, let me ask you this. There's been discussion that young writers in writing programs are too isolated, that they're not reading anything except the stories of their peers. I heard that you preferred teaching two classes, one of outside reading and one of writing.

That's what I liked. Otherwise your students get sucked into the vortex of self-absorbtion and competition with peers and "What's being published that's doing well?" and "How can I write something like that?" I think you must know literature, all the way back. I find even today the more I learn about good writers from the past, the better my writing is. And also, I'm always having to go out into other fields in order to bring my characters the lives they need to make them express what I feel moved to express. Religion . . . law . . . once even entymology, the study of bugs! You can't make all your characters come from the same environment you do and have them know only what you know. You just can't.

Q: You need something besides the inward search?

Oh, yes. If I were teaching on a regular basis again I would try to cultivate a mind-set in the young person, and the mind-set would be very simple: Paying attention, paying attention to what you are doing, knowing the names for things, knowing the names of weeds, for instance, getting everything you can out of everything you know. Because if your mind is at all an associative mind, and I believe a capacity for associations can be developed, then stories come out of this, plots come out of this, you get to know people better, simply by paying attention to what's before your eyes.

Q: In your essay on diaries ["A Diarist on Diarists"], you write that "fiction organizes the clutter of too many details into some meaning." But how as a teacher did you go about teaching the organization of those details, once observed? How did you help a student make sense of what they see?

You encourage selection. I wish I could think of an example. What detail is going to tell you more about the character, move the story along; what detail, of itself—if you're working on a big level—can stand for the reason behind that story? There's that nice literary term, "objective correlative." It isn't very descriptive; maybe we need another term. A detail, an object, something that will say, "This is the essence of the story." The famous one that is given in many creative writing classes is from *Madame Bovary*. On the way home from the first big party they went to, a nobleman flings a silk purse down on the road—am I remembering this right?—and Charles finds it and takes it into the carriage with him, and then she holds onto it and studies it and cherishes it and it becomes for her a physical symbol of the life she wants and cannot have. One detail like that—sometimes you can't look for it, it just makes itself known as you work on your story—becomes significant and helps the reader know what the story is, and what their angle on it is.

Q: Which leads me to ask about the larger framework in your fiction, through which these details are filtered. Your characters, on the one hand, seem individual and separate. At one point Margaret Gower says, "Does one ever really know anyone else?" And yet they are also connected in larger ways. In your diary essay you write, "We get unedited glimpses of the self in others, others in the self." How do you help a student get from the individual character to a connection with others? Or don't you try, because it's so much a personal choice?

Here, let me read you this. [Reads from a work in progress.]

"There are some things I liked about this piece of writing, but it's not a story yet," Hugo told the scruffy young man slouching in the chair. "You need to think it through a little more."

"What makes you say it isn't a story?"

"Well," said Hugo, "because nothing happens. What you've got here is basically just a meditation on . . . on a son's anger at his father. But, now, the zoo details are good. . . ."

The zoo details weren't all that good, but Hugo felt obliged to offer *some* encouragement. The more hopeless a student was, the kinder Hugo tended to become.

The boy said, "I wouldn't say the son was *angry*. He's more, like, *disillusioned*. And I don't agree with you that nothing happens. He's gone to the zoo, trying to recapture important lost feelings from his early childhood, and who does he see there but his father, playing with the back of some woman's *neck*. He discovers his father has a mistress. Are you saying *that's* nothing happening?"

The boy's voice rose, aggrieved far beyond the pitch neces-sary for defending his slight effort. He narrowed his dishwater-colored eyes at Hugo: slits of impotent wrath. This boy actually did see his father at the zoo, playing with the back of some woman's neck, thought Hugo, and it's the most important awful thing that's happened to him so far. And I'm the stand-in for the perfidious father as we sit here for the next twenty minutes and discuss it as a literary problem.

"No-no-no. By nothing happening, I mean. . . ." Hugo cracked his knuckles, an old bad habit when stalling for time. He wished he were more facile with this technical talk: it was one thing to feel your way through your own fiction; another thing entirely to locate where someone else had gone wrong. "Look," he said, "I'll try to clarify. I'm not saying the son has to stride around to the other side of the gorilla cage and punch his father out."

The responding gleam of animation in the boy's sullen face was not lost on Hugo.

"Or," said Hugo, "to go to the other extreme, I'm not saying that the father and son and mistress all have to go off and eat ice cream together and come to respect one another's points of view. I don't mean that, either. When I say nothing happens, I mean nothing happens to the reader. The reader's feelings haven't been moved, or his perceptions significantly changed, because he hasn't been given enough to work with. Now, a more skillful writer would be able to take the same incident and move or shake the reader through, oh, any number of tech-niques. Sheer evocative language alone, if you happen to be that kind of writer. . . ."

The dishwater eyes were fixed morosely on something, or nothing, on the mostly empty shelves behind Hugo.

". . . Or, if you were another kind of writer," said Hugo, "what you might do is find connections within the information you've already given us and then set about making them resonate. . . ."

The boy clearly wasn't listening, but Hugo droned on anyway, simply for the satisfaction of working out his own thoughts on the techniques of writing.

"For example," he said, "you mention in passing in your story, a sad, mangy old gorilla. Well, you might take that demoralized old gorilla and use him as an emotional focus on the boy's part. It's too early in life for the boy in your story to sympathize with his father, that won't come 'til years later, if at all; perhaps not until he finds himself in the same circumstances as his father one day. Now that might make *another* story. But meanwhile you could do more with that old gorilla."

(That's a detail, the gorilla, you see.)

"You could use that mangy old fellow-mammal as a sort of safe deposit box for the boy's growing ability to empathize with other creatures outside himself . . . you could establish a mood between the two unhappy creatures, trapped in circumstances not of their own making, if you see what I mean."

Hugo labored on, feeling like a psychoanalyst posing as a creative writing teacher. [Ends reading.]

It's that sort of thing that I would do. You have to have a specific example even to talk about it, so if this boy, which I made up, had brought in such a story, I would go for some detail like that to help him get out of the literal autobiography and into the larger significance. I mean, there's a situation—it happens to be *his* situation but it has tendrils that connect people to other people and mammals to other mammals, situations to other situations. You find the right detail and make it resonate.

Q: I've heard that you like D. H. Lawrence and Henry James and Charlotte and Emily Brontë . . . and among more contemporary writers, Robertson Davies and John Fowles. All of them, not secretly, write novels peopled with characters. That's somewhat true of you as a writer also.

And getting more so.

Q: Why is that? Is it that feeling again for the interrelationship of groups of characters?

I have an answer and then there's this scholar, a Chinese woman, who's writing a book on me who has another answer that I hadn't thought of.

I had some interesting people here to dinner the other night. He's a psychiatrist, she's a physicist, and they've written a book called *The Quantum Self* about the connections and concepts between what we know now about the physical world through quantum physics and how you can apply that to human relationships. This is a very intelligent man—years and years ago he was my second husband for a while; I met him at a creative writing course at the City Literary Institute—and they were talking about this, the way particles that are people interact. In the book I'm writing now there are four characters, all equally important, two men and two women, and they all change each other a great deal. They're not even close friends, but they change each other by being in one another's lives at a crucial time.

Now, what Emily Brontë did in *Wuthering Heights* was rather wonderful. What she was really doing with all these characters was working out her soul. She was a very interior person. Some of the characters die off, but there's a human wholeness at the end that came out of all this turmoil. Oh, here's something else. [Finds a note in a journal.] "The novel can teach us something no other form can about people. The imagined possibilities of people through the combining of individuals we know."

Now, the Chinese woman who is writing about me, she uses a theory of a Russian critic called Bakhtin—do you know the name?—and his theory I recognize instantly. [Gets up to look for a book.] Oh, where is that thing on Bakhtin? Here. I'll read this over twice, it's so important: "A diversity of individual voices when artistically organized, an interaction of diverse consciousnesses and voices among the individual self"—get that, *among* the individual self—"as well as among discrete individuals, constitutes the most important act of self-understanding." That's what I'm after. A diversity of individual voices . . . and then you have an interaction of diverse consciousnesses and voices all in the same person; in other words they're all in me, I'm making all these people out of my experience and the people I know and what I don't know. This interaction, as well as the one among discrete individuals, you and me, the different people in the book, constitutes the most important act of self-understanding.

And then there's George Eliot, another of my mentors. [Goes to get *Middlemarch*.] Dorothea is probably at the unhappiest point of her life because she has just discovered that the man she loves, young Ladislaw, is in the arms of the doctor's wife. Let's see if I can find this. When I read this I thought, oh, yes, this is the way I want to live and this is the way I want to write. OK, so first of all she's thinking how unhappy she is, and then she thinks, well, but it's not just me, there's me, and then there's Ladislaw, and the doctor, and the doctor's wife, Rosalind, and "What sort of crisis might not this be in three lives whose contact with her laid an obligation on her?"

And then she asks, "What should I do, how should I act now this very day if I could clutch my own pain and compel it to silence and think of those three?" And then: "It had taken long for her to come to that question and there was light piercing into the room. . . . She was a part of that involuntary, palpitating light, and could neither look out on it from her luxurious shelters a mere spectator, nor hide her eyes in selfish complaining." She suddenly opens.

Q: Like the epigraph in Forster's Howard's End.

"Only connect. . ."

Q: Unlike the stereotype people have of the Beckett figure, the lost singular soul wandering off. It's a choice writers make whether to add themselves onto others or strip down to nothing, isn't it—for young writers as well as older ones?

Some contemporary writers take as much as possible out of their work. But then there are others who open up, put in, keep putting in. Some people are not even taker-outers, it's never been in.

Q: Not a case of editing and editing down to a spare, bare minimum.

That's what I think Beckett was after. I think he was concerned with the human condition and he had gotten into a kind of creative despair where he decided, "I'm going to take everything out and start with the garbage pail and see what can be said." But I think some copycats just start with the garbage pail because they think that would be either like Beckett or because they want to do something a little shocking.

Q: The style of nihilism without the. . .

Nihilism without content.

Q: Without the path to it.

And without the genuine despair. Beckett had it and made it work for him.

Q: Let me get to the question of journal writing, which you are known for. Briefly, what does it give you, and then, in the context of the classroom, couldn't it be used? Did you ever try to get your students to do it?

Well, let me start with the students first. There's one thing that gives me the willies, which is to think about a teacher going in and saying, "Now we're all going to keep a journal all week and then we'll read our entries aloud." That's not a journal! Or these writers who write their journals and then publish them and start the next one. A journal is a dialogue with the self, and then it becomes a dialogue with the selves. It's a way to keep track of where you've been and who you were, it's a way to keep yourself honest. It can also be a form of prayer. Prayer is a way of conversing with an other, an other that's not you, not God in myself but an Other. The journal can be that, too. When I write in my journal I'm not just writing back at me, I'm justifying the day, and I'm asking questions, and I'm going on intellectual sorties without having to worry about sounding silly. It's very important to me but I wouldn't want to assign my students one to write and I certainly wouldn't want to read their journals. That's an invasion. And if anybody reads mine, they aren't around long.

Q: In what way is it useful to you, then, as a writer?

It's my underpinning from day to day. For instance, I've been writing this novel for over a year and without my underpinnings it would be so complex, I'd have to start reading it over every morning. So I keep track of myself from day to day. I have old journals and all these systems. These [points to a pile of about six leather-bound volumes] are just the ones I'm using for what I'm doing right now. I have systems with red ink and stars and drawings with light bulbs. They all make sense to me: Light bulbs mean I've just had this flash; stars, depending on how many, are something important; red ink means it definitely can go into the book; black ink is for my own thinking.

Q: Is there an energy that might be lost in the diary writing that could be put directly into your fiction?

I don't know, I can't even imagine. I do detect sometimes in the journal a kind of manic reckless energy, which comes from the fact that I can say it and don't have to be held accountable. So perhaps something is lost there. But sometimes I just transfer it in. I started a chapter the other day and the first words were perfect for this character, and they came right out of an entry in a journal. But they fit.

Q: I honestly don't know how many young writers would do it.

Well, also, I'm not living and working in some exciting place and worrying about finding the right man, and all that stuff. I live a very quiet life up here. It's almost a contemplative life. I've wanted it that way. I write my novel in the morning and do what I want to in the afternoon, and I write in my journal. A lot of young writers have jobs, they have a hectic social life or not enough social life, they're climbing and grabbing and holding on and sinking back and all those things. But of course when I was in my twenties, climbing and grabbing and sinking and yearning, I still did keep a journal. I have them all. At that time it was to record feelings and ideas. I actually made a novella out of some journals from the early sixties. *Mr. Bedford and the Muses* was about some young professionals who live in a boarding house in London. But I wrote my journal in those days just to keep myself sane. I was beset by existence, it was too much. You had to make a living and you had to be attractive, and you had to compose yourself, conduct yourself, all these things.

Q: Last question. Do you still have the urge to teach?

Teaching was very exhausting, but there are moments when it's elating, when you help someone or when someone comes in with a wonderful story and you get to ask them how they did it, when you talk like fellow writers. "Well, how many drafts did you go through, what was it like when you started, it didn't start like this, did it?" And you come to be craftsmen sharing secrets. I sometimes have urges to teach again. I reread a book that I love, *Portrait of a Lady*, and I suddenly wanted to go through it with others, because now I know more reasons why it's good and I want to share them.

John Irving

Born in Exeter, New Hampshire, in 1942, John Irving sold his first story while still in college and his first novel, *Setting Free the Bears* (1968), during his years as a student at the University of Iowa Writers' Workshop. There have been six novels since, including *The World According to Garp* (1976), *The Cider House Rules* (1985), and *A Prayer for Owen Meany* (1989), all commercial and critical successes worldwide.

Having taught at Iowa, Mount Holyoke College, Brandeis University, and elsewhere, Irving left university teaching in search of "always more time" to write. In these pages he expresses what he and not a few others have found as some of the inherent limits of formal teaching. He also vividly describes some of the many challenges the craft of writing presents to the young writer: the constant need for revision, for production ("Writing is like working out; you have to build up to your capacity, and then go beyond that"), and for the relationship to potentially distractable readers. He also speaks about the "obvious but painstaking" components of good fiction, namely "the craftsmanlike quality of the storytelling ... the true-to-life quality of the characters ... and the meticulous exactitude of the language" (from his essay "Getting Started").

John Irving lives in both Vermont and Toronto. He is a recent recipient of Officier des Arts et des Lettres of the French government.

Q: You studied writing at the University of New Hampshire as an undergraduate, and then at the University of Iowa Writers' Workshop, which especially then had the status as a young writers' mecca. Looking back, were there particular teachers or experiences of learning, in either place, that had special meaning for you as a developing writer?

Nowadays, I think, people do "study" writing. I never did, except in the sense that writers study what they read. I read the authors of the nineteenth century with the most eagerness, and I think I accomplished much of my learning from them. Dickens, Turgenev, Hardy, Hawthorne, Tolstoy, George Eliot; later Flaubert and Thomas Mann. Melville only a little. The twentieth century is not exciting to me, with the notable exception of Graham Greene; among living authors, I like Robertson Davies, García Márquez, Günter Grass. But I went to Iowa because it was a way to have time to write; period. I didn't want a job; I wanted to write. I got a so-called teaching–writing fellowship, or else I wouldn't have gone, and so I had a little money coming in and *lots* of time. At the University of New Hampshire I was fortunate enough to be encouraged by the writers John Yount and Thomas Williams; they impressed upon me that no one was going to "teach" me how to write—I just had to give it the time. Naturally, it helped to have an older, more confident writer reading over my shoulder—sometimes saying no more than "I like this," or "I don't like this very much." But I found that I needed that very little by the time I got to Iowa, and that led me to someone who *did* very little or almost none of that as a teacher—namely, Kurt Vonnegut. He said, "This part bored me." And then, one hundred pages later, he'd say, "This was really funny." Sometimes he said, "You certainly like *this* word a lot, don't you?" Mostly, he just let me be.

Tom Williams sent my undergraduate short stories to his agent, Mavis McIntosh. She took me on and sold one story before I graduated from college; then she retired and passed me on to a younger agent in her agency, so that my old friend and literary agent, Peter Matson, never really picked me, nor did I pick him. We were passed on to each other. (Peter now represents only my screenplays, as my novels and other literary endeavors are represented by my wife and agent, Janet Turnbull, but Peter remains my longest literary business relationship and I was very lucky to meet him.) Peter Matson sold *Setting Free the Bears* when it was only one-third complete (to Random House), and so I had a novel sold while I was still a student at Iowa, which gave me a lot of encouragement and confidence. Another advantage: I had a child when I was still an undergraduate. Either I went out to a job, or to wrestling practice, or I was at home writing, or I was with my kid. I was not very social at Iowa, and (as a consequence) I got a lot of work done.

I've always gotten a lot of work done. I write as much as I can every day. I don't care for everything Trollope wrote, although I love some things, but I greatly admire his writing habits. Writing is like working out; you have to build up to your capacity, and then go beyond that. And you have to keep doing that, again and again. My habits as a wrestler (I competed until I was thirty-four, and coached the sport until I was forty-seven) have given me more reliable tools as a writer than anything I "learned" at either New Hampshire or at Iowa. But, importantly, I was encouraged at both places, and by writers I much respected; that certainly helps. An early acceptance of a first novel also helps.

Q: In your experience as both student and teacher, in what way— through what means—is a good class made "good," when all is said and done? Is it through a general ambience of open and shared learning, the presence of a powerful personality or mentor, a teacher with good one-on-one editing skills? Something more?

I never edited student work. If a writer is ever going to develop, he must learn to edit himself. Not that a good editor, finally, isn't important, but the products of too many creative writing programs always look to me *in need of* editing. As a teacher, I used to carve *one* paragraph to pieces, and edit *it*; or with a single passage of dialogue—the same thing. But only as an example of a standard of precision that the writer must apply to himself. I sometimes would pass something back and say, "Show it to me in one month—not before." Revision is essential.

I spend four years writing a novel, but sometimes the first draft is finished in less than two years. I spend much more time rewriting than I spend writing. The clarity of the language is everything. Writing workshops that emphasize the need for revision are vital; but writing teachers and your fellow students can't do it for you, nor should they try—*except* as an example. Without self-criticism, everything looks like a first draft. And there aren't as many editors in publishing as there used to be; almost no one will edit a first novel. What they want is a *finished* first novel. And that is another mistake young writers make; they show first-draft work to publishers and agents. First impressions are the strongest. When I sold *Setting Free the Bears* on the basis of one-third of the novel, it was a *finished* one-third; it was rewritten on rewritten, and when the book was completed, I went back and revised that first third again, but there was very little that needed to be done to it. I revise as I go along, *and* after the whole. You can't revise enough. I stop reading most published books because I encounter some slack passage, some lame transition, some whimsical chapter break—something simply hasty, simply lazy. I sometimes wonder if the writer re*read* his own book, much less rewrote it.

Q: Do you think there should be a goal of a formal writing program such as Iowa beyond producing writers good enough to publish? Wallace Stegner said that "a writer must have a clear conception not only of self, but of the society." Since your novels often deal, sometimes explicitly, with social issues, is this outward-looking view something you tried to convey to your students?

Well, another much-discussed sin of writing-course novels is that they're about nothing, or rather that they're autobiographical novels about young people struggling to be writers. A mistake, of course. I was so afraid of that the first time that I wrote a historical novel about two *Austrians*! (Of seven novels, three have been historical, possibly to avoid as much as possible the autobiographical mistake; use your imagination, *not* your life. Life is too sloppy for good fiction. What we remember is a grocery list, not *selected*; if you make up the details, you must select them. Memory is too loose a tool for writing good fiction.)

I don't know that I subscribe to Mr. Stegner's thesis that it is "society" that the writer must know something about; certainly, that would be preferred. But I think simply the knowledge of *characters* who are utterly not yourself is vital; other people, people who aren't you. You must be able to characterize, and how can you do that if you don't know any people—*real* people? Of course, one valuable source of "real" people, for me, was really good novels. I know more about the characters in really good novels than I know about most people I know. I suspect that I know many Emma Bovarys, but none as well as I know *the* Emma Bovary.

Q: In the introduction to the Bantam edition of Great Expectations, *you wrote, "In the present, post-modernist praise of the* craft *of writing—of the subtle, of the exquisite—we may have refined the very heart out of the novel." Were you speaking about critics mostly, or are teachers of fiction today also culpable in emphasizing craft over the development of emotional value in their students' writing? Is emotion one of the things a student can (and should) work on in the writing classroom?*

No, emotion cannot be worked on in a classroom, but its absence (in a piece of writing) can certainly be noted. I had a student at Iowa who wrote a story about a dinner party from the point of view of a fork. Well, yes: It was witty, and neat . . . and so on and so forth. But there was a foreign student in that class, and he knew better than to be taken in by this fork-story. His English was good, but still it was English as a second language, and he was far behind the other students in his grasp of the language, and for this they condescended to him, heartily. But in this instance he silenced all their praise, which was unanimous, of the fucking fork-story. I hadn't yet said a word. I was groping. I wanted to say, "Trivial beyond compare!" I wanted to say, "Where are the *people* in this story?" But the foreign student beat me to it.

He said: "Excuse me, please, but is anyone in the class, unbeknownst to me, an actual fork? Is there another fork here?" There was sneering, but silence. And then the foreign student said: "If the fork in this story *died*, would any of us care?"

You must write about people who touch the reader; you must make the reader *care*. But why is this always put *in comparison to* craft? Craft is *also* essential. When I said "refined," in my reference to postmodernist, minimalist writing, I was not praising craft; by "refined" I mean that the minimalist story is so boiled down as to be boiled away; that in such a terse reduction of language (and of characterization and of plot and of emotion), there is nothing left but this tidy, self-conscious stance of the writer examining himself. Honestly, if you *could* develop character, and if you *could* imagine a great plot, a complex and interwoven story, and if you *could* be moving, why wouldn't you? Perhaps, if you lacked the ability to do these *essential* tasks of the nineteenth-century novel, you would then produce some lame little thing and claim it was your *choice* to write this way, and that you were *not* writing this way by default. In my view, such writing is by default.

Q: As a teacher, at Iowa and elsewhere, you must have had students influenced by, even trying to imitate, your style of writing. One teacher has said that, in the early eighties following the success of The World According to Garp *and* Hotel New Hampshire,

*many students of his were producing stories with bears and dogs.
Is this necessarily a problem? Is imitation an allowable, even
desirable, step toward the writer's own way of seeing? How far as a
teacher would you let it go?*

I stopped teaching after *The World According to Garp* was published because I no longer needed to teach; I could support
myself by my writing alone, and I wanted more time to write—
always more time. So I didn't experience *Garp* imitators in the
classroom. Certainly, however, I imitated Kurt Vonnegut in *Setting Free the Bears.* And certainly a novel as recent (of mine) as
A Prayer for Owen Meany is in part written in homage to *The Tin
Drum* and *A Christmas Carol* (and, I suppose, the New Testa-
ment, which is an awfully good story.) But I don't *write* like Vonnegut or Grass or Dickens; I borrow qualities, even priorities,
which were theirs. Isn't that what writers do? Of course, those
writers who have nothing of themselves to bring to their work,
or are only imitating style or gesture . . . well, they won't write
very well or very much, anyway, will they? Who said . . . "a fire
in the belly" . . . do you know this phrase? Well, you have to be
passionate about something. A woman, a man, a child, a tree, a
whole landscape, a street, an event in the past, a coincidence, an
accident . . . something or someone must be an *obsession.*

I don't write to tell my friends what they already know. I write
to a stranger, someone who I imagine is a hyperactive child;
much smarter than me, but more restless, and not very disci-
plined. And they're very busy, they have a much more interesting life than I have, they have much more to do than I have, and
my book must simply *seize* their attention and *keep* it, or I'll lose
them . . . and they'll never come back to my book because they
have so many other, more interesting entertainments all around
them and in their fascinating lives. *That* is the reader: a genius,
but a hyperactive child. Students putting bears and dogs in their
stories are imitating the wrong things. What they have to put in
their stories is a *compelling* reason for the reader to keep read-

ing. One such compelling reason is to care about what happens to the main character; simply that.

Q: With what kind of student did you make the most progress as a teacher? A writer like T. Coraghessan Boyle, a student of yours at Iowa, must have brought, even then, a natural linguistic flair to his work; others were perhaps more tentative. Do different talents offer different challenges?

You don't do anything with good students; you just encourage them, you tell them what they really (internally) already know or sense about their gifts, and sometimes you point out a habit—maybe a slightly irritating device that keeps recurring. They'll probably just smile and keep the habit. Cocteau said of his critics that one should pay close attention only to what they most dislike; that which they most dislike, he said, is probably the only original quality you have going for yourself, and you'd best make note of it and keep doing it and doing it.

Tom Boyle or Ron Hansen surely didn't learn much from me; I read them closely and let them know I was enthusiastic, and hip to their choice of detail. I flattered them. Remember: I was a wrestling coach a lot longer than I was a teacher. The advantage of coaching is plain. You have constant reinforcement to the criticisms you offer. If you tell someone he has a very vulnerable stance on his feet, or that he is a sucker for a side-roll in the top position, you are instantly backed up by his upcoming experience. He will go into a match, or even a practice session, and promptly be taken down, repeatedly, and he will be side-rolled over and over again. He'll come back to you, later, and say, "Uh . . . what was it you were saying about that side-roll?" But there's no backup to teaching writing; some of the worst stuff gets published, even praised. You can only say, "In my *opinion*, this is weak, this is poor, this is boring." . . . There is simply no equivalent to teaching a student a proper side-roll, or a proper defense against it.

I guess that's why I continued to coach wrestling, even after I could afford not to, and why I stopped teaching writing as soon as I didn't need to. No backup. And the worst part of teaching writing is that there is no advice you can give the *untalented* person, short of eventually making him a better reader—the end result of which will be that he'll become depressed about his own writing. That's the difficulty; good writers you can't help— you can only encourage them—and poor writers, you can't help either . . . you can only discourage them. This is vexing. I liked coaching because the *un*talented people found out what they lacked from other sources, from their opponents . . . *you* didn't have to rub their weaknesses in their faces; someone else did this. You could continue to be kind and encouraging; they learned anyway. And with good wrestlers, you could concretely teach them things to make them better; you could always find something they hadn't seen or didn't know, and they could learn it. It was very satisfying.

I take enormous pleasure in Tom Boyle's success, and in Ron Hansen's, but not because I contributed to their success; just because I knew them when they were young, and I became fond of them, and wished the best for them, and now I'm happy for them. But when a kid you are coaching wins a tournament or even just one difficult match, you can see *your* contribution— you can sometimes see *your* move, and better done than *you* ever could have done it. Two of my sons have won New England wrestling championships, a title that eluded me. There is no comparable gratification to "teaching" anyone writing. Most wrestling coaches I know are happy people; they love what they are doing. Most people I know who teach writing would rather be "just writing"; this is not to say that many of these teachers don't take their writing *and* their teaching seriously. But what writer wouldn't want to write full-time? ⌐ me

Q: Much of today's fiction tends to focus on bracketed moments in the lives of central characters, sometimes a few days, rarely more

than several years. Yet your novels draw characters from birth to maturity, in notable cases death, too. In The Cider House Rules, *for instance, we see the ways in which orphan Homer Wells can't control "the calendar of his life." You've written how important David Copperfield's question is: "Whether I shall turn out to be the hero in my own life, or whether that station will be held by anybody else. . . ." These are issues, often, of broad novels. Is narrative drive of the kind necessary for expansive writing something you tried to teach? Can it easily be taught, or does it fall in the domain of a more personal worldview?*

Ah, now *there's* a question! Yes, yes, and yes! Birth to maturity, the passage of time, the novel of the broad scope. Yes; it is the novel I most admire, and try to write. I feel I have best accomplished this with the last two (*Cider House* and *Owen*). Narrative drive is a good way to put it, or narrative momentum—it is essential in any novel longer than 125 pages (the length of an average screenplay). You, the reader, must be more interested on page 300 than you were on page 100 or else you won't keep reading; and by page 500, you must be *dying* to find out how all these strings are going to be tied, and how all these balls that have been thrown into the air are going to be caught. Narrative is like juggling: the more objects, the better; the more complicated and hard to catch, better yet. That is why the phrase "minimalist," as applied to novels, makes me laugh or throw up—or both. A minimalist novel; now what is that? A juggling act with one orange? Or perhaps the juggler only *imagines* that he has an orange. It's ridiculous. Let painting be minimalist, let gardens be minimalist, but not novels. Let them be as big and complex as the author can handle. And no, it can't be taught; scope is a matter of talent and taste. When I want to lose weight, I eat less—not worse. The minimalist novel is the *nouvelle cuisine* of literature; it's safe food (or writing) for people who lack discipline. But I was always very supportive of those students who wrote the tiniest short stories and *wanted* to write only the tiniest short stories; you can't be proselyte-hunting in the classroom. I save it for my friends.

Q: Do you miss teaching?

Do I miss teaching? What do you think? Emphatically, no! I miss coaching. I don't miss wrestling; I don't want to wrestle anymore—and, at fifty, I would be crazy if I did want to wrestle anymore. But I do miss coaching, for all the reasons stated. And I don't miss teaching . . . for all the reasons stated.

Gordon Lish

Gordon Lish, while still in his teens, had a career as a radio broadcaster, actor, and disk jockey. As an editor at Alfred A. Knopf (since 1977) and of the literary magazine *The Quarterly*; as the author of five novels (including *My Dear Mr. Capote*, 1983), three collections of short fiction, and many essays and edited anthologies; and as a teacher of one of the most well-known independent writing classes in the country, his name today is recognized on three fronts. His activities in and around teaching, especially, have been the subject of scores of newspaper and magazine articles, many quite recent.

Still, writers, editors, teachers, and students of writing who may know his name or have heard of marathon seven-hour classes may know much less of his actual teaching methods and the theories underlying them. In the following conversation, Gordon Lish discusses an array of subjects, among them the immortality of art, the seduction of the reader, the composition of sentences, and the ardor needed for a writing life, his own and his students'. "The only way one can keep on," he says here, "as Picasso kept on, as Degas kept on, as no few artists do keep on . . . in the face of every kind of reason to succumb, is to find in the will, in desire, a superior response."

Gordon Lish has taught at Yale, Columbia, and New York universities. His most recent works are the novel *Zimzum* (1993) and *Ten Bits* (1993), a collection of short fiction. In the spring of 1993 he was awarded an honorary doctor of letters degree from the State University of New York.

This conversation took place in New York City, which is the site of his independent classes.

Q: Let me begin by asking you how the students in your classes are selected.

Well, almost entirely on the basis of will. Desire. If I have one place left, and there is a student who will fly in from Portland, Oregon, a student who will move to New York for three months, a student who will commute back and forth to Chicago, as against a student who will roll out of bed and take the bus across town, I'm likely to take the one who will undertake the greater inconvenience. I'm willing to believe that everything depends upon ardor, on will, on desire, on resolve. And if the student can demonstrate that resolve by his statements, by his acts, as against that student who fancies himself very gifted, very talented, I'm going to bet on the hungrier of the rat.

Q: What does "will" mean, in the context of writing?

Will is everything. Desire is everything. In this activity and in life. One must want, and want so greatly, that every sort of impediment is only another occasion for the determination of the student to seek its solution, and in such solutions finding new prospects for problems further on. Everything wants your failure. The body that you inhabit, the time that is yours, the circumstances of your life, every particularity that can be summoned to the general spectacle of your enterprise through space and time, can be seen as an interference to doing great art—nothing more efficiently than the mortality that is your due. And to exert ceaselessly in the face of such circumstances is to require an exorbitant desire. One must want so greatly that every reason to succumb is dismissed.

As one goes forward making the composition, one is always establishing a move, a gesture, a decision, an election that defeats what has been offered up by the composition itself. One is engaged in a kind of global and rapid-fire problem-solving procedure that might be seen as offering moves against moves. For every move that is made, there is a countermove.

Well, likewise, as composition is done, so is done the life which encompasses the artist. One is certain to be continually offered up by experience reasons to quit, reasons to turn back and start anew. One will be shown why one is insufficient, incompetent to proceed. And in order to proceed, one must continually mount solutions—resolutions in the case of living one's life—against those impediments. One has to *earn* one's life as an artist.

In my own life now, for example, I am confronted with enormous personal difficulties in the context of my family, my income getting and the like. Everyone who does life, as against resigning from life, will be constantly caught up in contest with an array of impediments. Eventually we are all entirely surrounded by circumstances which want our defeat and which invade ever more persuasively toward that end. As one ages, one is certain to find that the body is increasingly going to announce its villainy. The only way one can keep on—as Picasso kept on, as Degas kept on, as no few artists do keep on, as Stephen Hawking, the cosmologist, kept on and kept on in the face of every kind of reason to succumb, is to find in the will, in desire, a superior response.

Q: But aren't you also assuming a level of artistic talent on the part of the writer?

No. No, I don't see a connection. And as a matter of fact in my own instruction as a teacher of writing—although my concerns are specifically the production of prose fiction, the enabling of my students to produce literary artifacts of a kind that invite the attention of history—I nevertheless feel required to oblige them to consider the totality of the problem that confronts them. It is not enough to be adroit at the composition of sentences; one must be adroit at living a life in the face of the prospects of defeat. I know so many young persons—no, I know so many *persons*—marvelously endowed, who are so deprived of an effective reckoning with the life problem that they have either abandoned the activity or let the activity decline and decline, to the point where it is at a great remove with history's concerns.

So that I don't think that talent or gift, if such things do exist, has anything to do with what the final receipts will be. My notion is that anyone who speaks, by reason of that speech, has prospects of achieving important imaginative writing. I see the notion of talent as quite irrelevant. I see instead old-fashioned notions of perseverance, application, industry, assiduity, *will, will, will, desire, desire, desire.*

Q: Ninety-nine percent perspiration, one percent inspiration?

Absolutely, absolutely. And I think it is not at all difficult to state the matter that simply. Everything is will and the great obstacle is always fear. It comes down in every instance to this dualism between what one wants and what one may be afraid to have.

Q: Before asking you about the actual method of composition you teach, I'd like to touch briefly on the question of academic writing programs.

Well, I can't really claim to be informed. I have very slight knowledge of what in fact obtains in the formal programs where one matriculates for a master of fine arts, until there are even some schools now that offer doctoral degrees in imaginative writing. Absurd on the face of it. But there may be in fact profit for people who pursue such degrees. I can only speak to my own program, which of course as you know is entirely without any kind of formal procedures and lacks certainly the formal evidence that is present in a university setting. I can't give a degree and I can't give a certificate. I can only offer my own exertions in the matter, which tend to be—I understand from those who have experienced both the formal setting and my own—rather exorbitant.

Q: You taught at Yale.

I taught at Yale, at Columbia, at N.Y.U., and I don't think whatever criticism I might want to assign to those settings is necessarily the fault of the setting itself or the setting itself susceptible to some kind of defect. People are people, they do what they will do in whatever setting you put them in. Certainly such observation is as appropriate for students as it is for teachers. Students who come to me, recognizing that they cannot at the end of their time with me point to a document which presumably entitles them to conduct professional activities of either a teaching or a writing kind, I think may demonstrate considerably more will and desire and *courage* than those who come away from the experience with a piece of paper in their hand. It may be that the very character of my classes in respect to what you *cannot* get from them creates a self-sorting process that delivers to me animated students.

Q: And as far as actual composition is concerned—if one could separate craft, style, language on the one hand, and content on the other, you have a strong view about the first part, the way sentences should be put together in writing. One of your students described your method as "walking backwards."

Yes.

Q: Unlike traditional narrative fiction.

My argument is that one can arrive at an enormously *more* effective artifact, that is, a storytelling act, if one is attendant upon a procedure called *recursion*, which means that in essence one finds one's utterance by reason of one's examination of what has *already* been uttered. The utterance that you are at this point embarking on takes its origin from what has just been stated prior to it. Traditional storytelling, or the art of storytelling, is rather more recursive than discursive, though I recognize there's not always a sharp line between them.

There's much more to this than what I've just stated, because one requires additionally the notion of *torque*, or what I sometimes call "the swerve," in order to bring about the arcs of the story. So that on the one hand one finds the origins for one's current utterance in what is prior, but one is always in a combative relation with what is prior. And this combat, this torque, must issue forth sentence by sentence by sentence or utterance by utterance by utterance. One can construe the parts of the composition as sentences if one wishes, or as paragraphs, or as other kinds of units, entirely depending on the steepness of the arc one is in search of.

I think, to put it as plainly as I might, the answers arrive out of examining what is prior and swerving from it. It is rather like the generation of a plant issuing from itself. At one point there was nothing there, and the singularity which set everything in motion from the seed, like the original singularity of the cosmos, contains within it the potentiality for everything that might issue forth: sentences, paragraphs, chapters, pages. Everything is dependent or contingent on what is prior. This arrangement of contingencies is in fact the narrative act. I'm giving it to you in the most simple-minded fashion, because there are sophistications in this procedure which can keep us seated here in an exchange for months without having touched the right ones.

Q: One wouldn't, putting it even more simply, know the plot before one started—one wouldn't have it worked out?

There is no plot. Plot is not a dishonorable concept. [But] we are talking here of the production of the kind of writing that stands the greatest chance of moving literary art forward on the great historical wheel of the national literature. We are not talking about creating product in the marketplace; we are not talking about getting published; we are not talking about anything other than how to come into possession of a totality, an utter totality, which seizes the attention of the best readers of your time.

I would want, since this is my time, to be read by Harold Bloom and Denis Donoghue and Julia Kristeva and a couple of dozen other persons whose names I could recite for you. And that would really be the only thing I would want. If I could seduce their attention into a rapture that I like to assign as "the gaze," I would feel I had done ably in enacting my art. I don't know very many better readers than Denis Donoghue or Harold Bloom or Don DeLillo or Cynthia Ozick. If I could manage to mount a succession of events that enforce "the gaze" in any of the persons just named, I would feel accomplished and pleased with my efforts and see them as having brought about the end that I wish for them, and that's all that I wish. The event of publication, the event of reviewing, all the rest of that fame, notice, is beyond the realm of my concern.

Q: So when you said earlier that you want to enable students to "invite the attention of history," what you mean is. . . ?

One can undertake every sort of recreative act in a hobbyist kind of way; one can go run around in the park in the expectation that one is going to keep his body furnished against the tide of time, but one knows that that is not possible to do. But in art, one likes to think, one is not subject necessarily to the incommensurate power of time. There are ways, I do think, to exert force, perhaps even commensurate force, against the exigencies of time and space. And it seems to me that the only reason to undertake an activity of such an entirely difficult kind is for the sake of history.

It must be very hard to run around in the park, you know, so many miles every day. It must be very hard; I've never tried it— I imagine it would be an unthinkable act to me, I couldn't run around the block—but those persons who can do this, say, who can run a marathon, must be persons of extraordinary zeal and absolute majestic resolve. I would answer, "For what?" In the end they are defeated. We're reduced to, in any event, simply drawing fictions against reality. I mean, all Stephen Hawking is doing as he comes into possession of some kind of cosmological structure is seeking to project a fiction that is continuous with his mind, and which reclaims his lost hegemony over reality. One is seeking, in the doing of prose fiction, the same kind of reclamation of hegemony over reality. One enters into a certain kind of concentration and projects a fiction, presumably, desirably, powerful enough to penetrate time and space. To undertake such a remarkable act for anything other than heroic reasons seems to me pointless. History is the only arena.

Q: Let me go back to the subject of composition, sentences and so forth. . .

Well, composition is really the only lie. The assembly of this succession of utterances is a lie. It is achieved by reason of an array of decisions that have nothing to do with what we would like to think of as the probity, the honesty, in the occasion. That is to say, the work is set in motion, by reasons of one's embrace of a right object. An entirely outrageous literary performer will prove to be reckless enough to embrace among his right objects the object that, at that moment in his experience, is his *rightest* object. Such an object is unique to himself and dangerously engaged. But that's the end of it. Once I have accomplished that reckless act into which one rushes forth by reason of one's audacity, that's an end of the irrational—and therefore the honest. All of that craft, all of that art, is empty of truth. It has as its teleology only the achievement of "the gaze" in the reader, at the expense of every other concern. The assembly, the composition, is a lie, from beginning to end.

Q: A willing lie, a knowing lie?

One is an idiot, one is a fool, one is a naif if one thinks otherwise. Doing great literary composition is an act for grown-ups, not for children, and one can perform these acts importantly only when one is entirely alert to every nuance of what is at issue in the making of composition. And one must be responsive. You're playing a game. Remember, I gave you the theme for this earlier. I said, there's a move for every move. Well, in fact, as you go forward in an act of composition, as you accrue sentences, accrue utterances, that theme becomes infinitely complex. There are an infinite number of moves for every number of moves. The artifact that you are struggling to achieve answers you at every unitary step with a widening array of moves. And you have to therefore find ever more complex solutions. So as the lie exfoliates, it becomes compounded exponentially and takes you farther and farther from anything that might be claimed to be honest, true. And this is a procedure of such startling difficulty that it could scarcely be accomplished with any deftness by someone who is unalert to what he was doing.

Q: And the result, I'm quoting some from you and your students, is writing that "sticks to the page"?

Well, someone may have produced a sentence which I regard as very breathy, not a voiced sentence, one in which there's a high incidence of unvoiced syllables, and I might say, "It's not really clamped to the page. It doesn't stick to the page." But that doesn't help us very much, does it? You have to first know what it is to produce a sentence that has in it a great deal of acoustical pressure.

Q: Would you say, though, that there is there a sound, a language quality among your writers?

No, no, no. There can never be. Well, I think I've heard it observed by impresarios who have arranged for my students to read somewhere that their prose seems remarkably spoken, remarkably musical, that the distinction between the writing my students and other persons perform was extraordinary. That there is a much more vocal and forceful effect delivered.

I can tell you why this is the case: A great deal of time is spent in my classes bearing in on what it is to create an acoustical event and how one parses out the properties of utterances. One then understands how they are to be manipulated in order to heighten the acoustical character of the sentence. My students become, if they're able, very deft at crafting sentences so that sensory effects of the most subtle kind are within their dominion.

You see, the task is really reducible to a few very plain statements. As I've said, there is a move for every move, and in recursive composition the moves one needs to consider exfoliate exponentially against the array of moves one can make as responses. One can also say that the prize goes to him who can control everything. We are talking essentially about an act whose success reposes entirely in the matter of control. Now, if I say to you, "Your job is to control everything that you have produced to the attention of the reader, to be in control, or to use Coleridge's expression, that you have 'invested your voice, your authority, in every phrase you have set down on the page,'" well then the question becomes: What is that "everything?" How much do you see? Are you concerned to know the sentence as a grammatic act, are you concerned to know the sentence as a syntactic act, how many ways can you begin to see what is present or potentially present in the office of the sentence? The more you know about the potentialities of sentences, the wider or bigger that "everything" is going to be for you.

Well, my job as a teacher, it seems to me, is to widen and widen my students' apprehension of what that "everything" is, and then give them the means by which to exert control over it. Now, obviously, I cannot enumerate all the conditions that will confront them as they do composition. If they're doing composition in the right kind of ways, conditions will be novel. And the solutions that will be adduced to their reckoning will have to be novel as well. But what I *can* do is to habituate them in the art of seeing and acting. I can establish their vision of what the composition is, and I can sharpen their possession of themselves as persons able to arrive at solutions for every potentiality. In the end the greatest artifact will be produced by that writer who has had most global control over his material. It therefore follows that I have to achieve in my students—since I want in them nothing less than the first prize—the powers of perception and of determination. That "everything" is in the vision of Dawn Raffel clearly larger than in the vision of her inferior. She sees more.

DeLillo and I say, when we chat in the little that we ever do about difficulties we are both confronting in our own work, that the more obdurate the wall one is facing, the more glorious will be the window one is able to produce in that wall, and the more fabulous will be the vista that one will then see. So one is always seeking.

I mean, it's all about how much you can possibly see, and how resolute you will be in seeking your answer to what is seen. Nothing is ceded; nothing is yielded. The story owns none of itself. You own it all. There is no story apart from your intervention; there never was. I'm told that Saul Bellow was once asked what Augie March would have to say in reflection on Reaganomics. My own reply, were I asked to sit as Bellow's coach on the matter, would have been: Tell them there is no Augie March. Tell them he is occasions of ink on a sheet of paper, and the personality they have come to imagine is a function of the arrangement of those occasions of ink on the sheet of paper. You have successfully achieved the projection of a fiction such that it penetrates time and space, and you've made believers, but they are fools, fools. The reader is present to the artifact only such that his seduction might be sought. One wants from him nothing more than his rapture.

You see, quite wonderfully, the greatest readers are also those who are most enraptured, should the artifact have the competency to prove that response in them. I recently read against my will Cormac McCarthy's *Blood Meridian*, and was enraptured, thoroughly his creature, so that even in the face of what I took to be McCarthy's failures of judgment, I was helplessly his creature. I cannot point to very many objects and artifacts of that kind in my recent life. It thoroughly seduced me despite every effort I had to resist it. I would regard it as a work of art of nothing less than surpassing power.

Q: In terms of the material from which students draw for their writing, you ask for a good deal of truth seeking.

Well, my position is entirely this: If great art were a function of great erudition, there'd be very little for what those of us who claim to be teachers to do. My own feeling is, as I remarked earlier, that the power of speech is ample for one's making the most heroic beginning so long as this power is wedded to equal possession of one's self, one's will, one's desire. The only source from which one can hope to achieve the seduction of history is what reposes in the self. This had nothing to do with education, nothing to do with erudition, nothing to do with reading an encyclopedia.

I ask my students to enter upon an examination of themselves in order to find those objects in themselves which have the greatest potency, a potency, should it be manipulated in a public setting, [that] might produce danger to their lives. By manipulating it in a public setting, they make themselves susceptible to every kind of harm; and this is where we begin. It is a psychoanalytic act which has in it no therapist. One is always in pursuit of tropes—symbols seen as objects which stand for other objects—and hoping to annihilate them by the act of writing, finding in fact what they were an evasion of—other tropes—and so on and so. And you are always many tropes behind yourself. But that's OK. Meanwhile you get an art out of it until you've worn yourself out. These are your materials.

Now I don't mean, in any of this, that one is in search of the abstract. On the contrary. For example, one's sense of mortality would never be acceptable as an object, but one's father's wristwatch might be, you see.

I give them to understand the shaman or the witch doctor, who presents himself to those foregathered for him. The witch doctor empties from the pouch he carries on his belt a piece of wingbone, a piece of shell, a pebble, a stick. It's like that. Now, what would be your pebble, your piece of broken bone? We all of us have a pocket, many pockets. I'm asking you to take out of your pocket those objects you're earnestly possessed of. And I'm not interested in students who promote fictions to begin with. I'm interested in the students who have the courage to actually empty out their handbags onto the table and say, "Well, you know I've got this battery here, I've a nine-volt battery." It's very different than saying, "I'm enraged with my husband; I don't like my husband because he's too short." No, "I have a nine-volt battery." The first sentence might in fact say, "This battery is possessed of nine volts of power." And the second sentence might say, "Had I a battery possessed of any fewer volts of power, it would be insufficient to do the job that this battery does." And so on. One would begin to weave his sentences, his utterances, in such recursive style until eventually perhaps engaging even *the meaning* of that nine-volt battery.

But I'm not interested in meaning. I seek in my students an appreciation for dearth of meaning. I'm interested in the seduction of the reader. Meaning is irrelevant. I am not interested in compositions which seek to uncover mysteries; I'm interested in compositions which seek to propose mysteries. A great writer need not be smart, he need only be clever. The witch doctor wants to continue on as the witch doctor; he wants to be assigned that role in the tribe the following season. That's all he wants, his continued hegemony over the tribe.

Q: In your observation of the learning curves of your students, as they work with sentences on the one hand, themselves on the other hand. . .

Which happens faster?

Q: Which happens faster and which kinds of students are able to do one and not the other?

Yes, very good question. You've asked me a question no one's ever asked me before. I can probably say with some vehemence—seeing my students through the other end of a telescope—that those who go on to have careers expressive of astonishing strengths of craft interest me much less than those who prove to have astonishing possession of themselves, of their evasions. It's lovely when one finds the wedding of the two, and then one has such a person as Dawn Raffel or Victoria Redel or Christine Scutt in my current class. Ben Marcus is a fellow who has colossal possession of the manipulations but probably rather less possession of his "objects"—or is launched, let us say, on a less audacious discovery of his objects. But of course Ben Marcus is twenty-four or twenty-five; Dawn Raffel must be thirty-five. So we are also speaking of abilities that have no little to do with where one is in life.

I will say something I feel required to say. I think in the main, my students, as they begin to make their way, are very inclined to drift from the more puzzling, the more arduous aspects of this activity, and to let it be filled up with easier objects. They find that their handiwork is so deft and at such a remove from those with whom they are competing that it's quite ample for them to make their way in the world. So that they do rather handily by simply being handy. Were I to have my way, I would prove able to build into them a more desperate relation to what I think is the moral work of being an artist.

At a certain part of my examinations of these matters I would have held Harold Brodkey aloft as easily our most interesting writer, and I continue to think that certain enterprises of his, in the collection *Stories in a Classical Mode,* are far and away the best things in the language. We don't have anything better than certain of Brodkey's stories, which I take to be the equal of the best novels we have. And I'm only satisfied with my students when they evince comparable relations to the moral work. When they fall from that difficult mark, then I am likely to be disappointed in them. Too many of my students let themselves be pried away from that moral work.

Q: While under your auspices?

No, afterward. No, under my auspices I think I rather keep them to the mark. I'm rather fussy about these things. I'm not easily pleased at all. And my students usually do want to please me.

It's hard to give you a picture of these classes. I mean, they're different in every instance—every class from every other class. For example, the classes I taught this summer were seven and a half hours long, and no one talked but myself. And it was a thoroughly enshrouding experience for all of us. It is not easy to be in such a setting and be unserious. You know, if you can sit seven hours without getting up to visit the facilities or to nibble at something, that's comparable to flying from New York to Vienna, for example, without getting up to relieve yourself. Well, my students do better than that, actually. So you would take them to be serious people, given to behaving in accordance with the most taxing material in the class, which is the moral material.

But once you are deprived of the office of such a setting [where] others are doing the same crazy thing and someone is hectoring you and hectoring you to meet some exorbitant mark all the time, once you return to the awful burden of your isolation, it may seem a lot more appealing to do a deft piece of composition than to begin a heroic piece of uncovery. So the moral work is the rather more perplexing of the two, and certain writers for whom I've had the highest hopes, the highest hopes, become diverted by the temptations of the marketplace.

Q: Which are ever-present?

Well, you see, I hope to impart to my students an indifference to the marketplace. Certainly you are right, the marketplace encroaches upon them as they begin to exhibit sufficient skill to get themselves in print; they are enticed away. They will publish with me, for example, an effective collection of stories, and the next thing you know someone has called up and wants to assign them the job of interviewing a bunch of Olympic swimmers, which has nothing to do with the art they have acquired. Certain ones of these persons will say, "No, I think not. This is not what I'm a writer for, it's not what I'm about." But others will be enchanted and distracted; they can now interview on assignment and the hell with sitting at home and writing fiction. I have seen this pattern quite a lot, and there will only be the few of them that will be able to resist such blandishment. Despite the strictness of my classes, despite the high order of the moral requirement, as it were, the bulk of them will very quickly be seduced away. It's a great sadness to me, a great sadness.

Not infrequently, I must also observe, once having let themselves be taken away, they find themselves wanting back in again and can't get back in again. It's impossible to ever forget the broad spacious grandness of the boulevards and the whiteness of the buildings. They just can't get back to their awful labors again.

To do composition in the terms I propose is to be solitary. That alone is more than they can bear. It means always to write against your time, it means to write outside your time, it means the instant you are claimed by official organisms to be a writer of a certain kind you are now obliged to move on to a new space. They don't want to do that. It's much easier to let themselves be typified and then work to a model that is successful in the marketplace. It's really the rare artist who is able to sustain an idea of himself as an artist, but this is true in every pursuit. It is scarcely no more the case in the literary arts than it is in any other kind.

And indeed, in this respect, we can properly encompass within the definition of artist anyone, in any practice, who undertakes that which has not been done before. In this context, Stephen Hawking is as much an artist as Albert Einstein was, as much an artist as Sigmund Freud was. Harold Bloom will continually insist these were our great poets. Sigmund Freud was a great poet; Karl Marx was a great poet. These are persons who projected great fictions onto the imagination of the world. That's what it is. But as history teaches us, it's a most discouraging labor, given that one, although he is working outside of time, is living in his time.

I have among my closest friends James D. Watson, who along with Francis Crick proposed the molecular structure of DNA. He and Crick worked in virtual isolation from the bulk of their fellows, single-mindedly engaged at the cost of the most exorbitant kind, reputation and the like. But what do they do lately? Have they been able to keep to such a mark over the course of their inventive lives, their intellectual lives? It's a lot easier to go to a party, a lot easier to be interviewed as I am letting myself be done now, than to be about my own solitary labors as a writer. It's easier to enact the pose in the context where one has one's audience than it is to do the work.

Q: One of your students told me that you considered teaching "a pure activity."

That's right. It's the purest thing I do.

Q: You think of yourself that way first, as a teacher?

Yes. I recognize in myself larger satisfactions from this activity than from all others that I've engaged. Furthermore, I am able to achieve more honesty in this activity than in any of the others. When I'm in a classroom, for that allotted time, I am closer to the truth of myself than I am in any other activity of my life. Whether professional or otherwise. I am more of myself as a teacher than I am as a writer or as an editor or as a husband or as a father or as a friend. The best of me, the most useful of me, is in evidence as a teacher. And I am as a teacher most alive to myself. So that I like myself in that context and find myself deriving from it more pleasure than I do in any other context. I come closer to getting myself shed of what I don't like about myself. And in fact, in this wise, teaching improves. Whereas contrastly, writing declines. I less and less like myself as a writer. I more and more see myself incompetent of escaping from my distractions.

Q: Your students know of your role as editor also. And in terms of The Quarterly, *there's a potential at least for those you like to be published.*

Yes, if I have taught someone to write ably I am not a little interested from profiting from that ability. It sometimes wounds me greatly when my students don't wish to have me publish them. They would sooner be published elsewhere. I find that sometimes very troublesome, very dismaying; I see it almost as a kind of disloyalty, but it happens a lot. Quite a lot. My students will say, "Well, gee, Gordon, I'm very pleased you want that piece but I'd sooner publish it in another literary magazine," for whatever reasons are at hand.

Q: Few have turned down a book contract, though.

That's a different thing. I think that has happened. I try not to let it happen because I try to be there from the first. They are emerging writers and I'm the one who's first aware of that emergence, and so I try to seize these people before anybody else can get their hands on them. In fact Anderson Ferrell represented a case of someone I seized with only one paragraph he'd written and I gave him a book contract based on that paragraph. It was a fine novel called *Where She Was*, and he's now engaged on writing a much finer novel, which I also have under contract.

But certainly if your question goes to the point that my students have an added cause of ardor in my case, given that I might act as an editor on their behalf . . . but then of course this really exists one way or another in no few writing classes, where the teacher may himself be under contract and tips off someone. One way or another I suppose it can be claimed that any student in any kind of formal setting anywhere, in a university or not in a university, is going to be in touch with somebody who has his hands in closer touch with the reins that can provide print.

Q: It may stir competition, but that may not necessarily be a bad thing?

But I'm all for competition. I can't get enough of it. I think that we are all of us, even in entirely isolated terms, engaged in a competition. Competition becomes the dynamic by which all growth takes place. It necessarily follows from the circumstance, one hardly has to inject it.

First of all, one necessarily seeks the approval of the teacher, the father, as is natural in the family romance. I am in that context the father. There is a person who is in authority and others who are seeking to have the approval of that authority. Even if I were to promote by words and deeds every air of cooperation, you can't empty the circumstance of that dynamic, nor would I want to.

I have taught creative writing for over thirty years. I have absolutely not the least doubt that those who prove best able to acquire the poetics that I'm promulgating are invariably those who are the most determined. And I've seen the other kind again and again. Highly verbal persons, they've been told their lives long that they should be writers, been told they've written beautifully and convinced themselves they've written beautifully, who prove not to have the moral bearing, at least in the circumstance of my class. I tend to be very suspicious of those who think themselves very greatly talented. And I tell them, "What do you want to come to me for? If you think you're writing beautifully now, what do you think I can add to that?" "Well, everyone says you're great." I say, "But my greatness resides really in my getting rid of everything you think is beautiful." No. I'm much more inclined to want to bet on somebody who is approaching these matters humbly and who sees themselves as virtually deprived, but who for crazy reasons wants to be a writer.

Q: Has your teaching changed over the years?

Every set of classes change and change. I think there's been a decisive strengthening of my teaching since my personal difficulties have become so considerable, as I expect I'm finding the need to take my happiness, such as it can be taken, from my classes.

And I've seen life play itself out in certain ways that convince me that art is the only escape. When there is no escape, art is the only pretense that has any durability to it. Other pretenses are too quickly doomed. Religion is certainly a conventional and successful answer, and the only one I think that answers the one that art makes. I don't see flight, I don't see drugs, I don't see the life of unreason as a successful enough reply. One must make a reply or one succumbs to the reality principle and surrenders early on, one becomes the living dead. So one makes a reply in fiction, or in art, and it occurs to me that *art* art, this art, real art, at least has the virtue of sustaining itself rather longer in time and rather more widely in space than others. It seems to me, anyway.

Q: This is really a first question, but who were your teachers? You've spoken of Edward Loomis.

Yes, yes. I only had one formal writing teacher. It was at the University of Arizona, and it was Edward Loomis. I think I lasted two or three meetings. I remember running from his class in what must have been barely contained tears. I know that when I returned home I surely dissolved into hysterics before my wife and children, feeling that I had been used badly by a bully, and of course the use he made of me was entirely for my own good and I was too little an artist to understand this. In subsequent years I came to be very disappointed in myself for not having proved to have the mettle to stand up to his extraordinary intellect and moral bearing.

So Loomis has had I think a not inconsiderable impact on my ideas of myself as a man first, and as a writer and teacher secondarily. I've learned more from his short story, "A Kansas Girl," about a life given over to service, to duty, to strictness, than I ever did in any writing class I had with him. Before that time I found myself powerfully taught by Poe, Joyce, Beckett, Emily Dickinson, Whitman, Emerson. I claim to have the greatest affiliation with certain European and Latin American writers. I find myself really willing to declare I never finished a single book by Borges, but I'm much enamored of the idea of such an affiliation. I really can't claim to having ever read a word of *Ulysses*, nor would want to, and yet I feel myself in certain ways the result of my *idea* of Joyce. I think Harold Bloom would claim that strong writers only read themselves, and that it is your misreading of your precursors that counts. So it is my misapprehension of Joyce, of Beckett. I can't deny that for three or four years of my life I virtually saw my walk as consonant with the walk I imagined James Joyce had. But I was probably more taught by Joyce's letters than I was by his prose fiction.

Today, every time I read DeLillo I learn from DeLillo, I learn from Brodkey, I learn from Ozick, I learn from any of the persons I admire. I probably can claim to learn the most from the last strong writer I read. So Cormac McCarthy has taught me the most.

Q: Just as you speak of your experience with Loomis, I would think perhaps there are some students who have not been prepared to profit from Gordon Lish.

Oh, I don't doubt there have been a lot of those! I think I have probably run off many more from my classes than Loomis has. I'm sure he's a much more tactful and gentle presence than anything I might claim to have been. I don't doubt that I have made many more enemies by reason of my teaching than I have made friends, and I really am willing, as painful as it is, to reckon with that as a citizen in the world. As a teacher I think I am probably achieved in this respect. I don't think any strong student should go away from a strong teacher feeling friendly to that teacher. I think he should be bent upon that teacher's undoing. Please God the student will have the grace and wisdom to know that the undoing should take place within the context of doing the prose fiction, not in sitting down and writing for a popular magazine a hatchet piece about his teacher. Not too many go away with that in mind. If they want to undo you, they call you at three o'clock in the morning and shriek into the telephone.

I don't doubt I've made a lot of unhappy persons in my classes. I can't say I'm sorry for that except insofar as it has abutted personal life. I don't like being made the object of assault in popular magazines. I do rather like a student who goes away determined to outwrite that son of a bitch eight ways to Sunday. That's swell, let him try.

Clarence Major

Born in Atlanta in 1936, Clarence Major grew up in Chicago. He graduated from the State University of New York, Albany, and received his doctorate from the Union Institute in Ohio. Among nine books of poetry and seven novels, he is the author of *My Amputations* (which won the Western States Book Award, 1986), *Such Was the Season* (a Literary Guild Selection, 1987), and *Painted Turtle: Woman with Guitar* (which was a *New York Times* notable book of the year, 1988). He has received wide recognition for his experimentation with and across fictional forms, including the novel, fable, and poem.

Clarence Major has taught both literature and creative writing at colleges and universities since 1968, among them Brooklyn College, Sarah Lawrence College, Howard University, the University of Washington, Seattle, and the University of Colorado, Boulder, where he taught for twelve years. He is currently director of the graduate program in creative writing at the University of California, Davis. In these pages he speaks of a consistently open approach to teaching writing, with no rigid style imposed on his students. In this regard, the importance of remaining open to influence is made clear: "Once you write a book, the experience of writing it will not in any way prepare you for the next one. It's always new, always fresh, always dangerous, always a struggle, word by word, step by step." He also speaks eloquently here of the great challenge for writers of all backgrounds to reach beneath a surface of culture, its "trappings and decorations, [in order to] tap into levels of human experience" to which all people respond.

Most recently, Clarence Major served as editor of the anthology *Calling the Wind: Twentieth-Century African-American Short Stories* (1993).

The University of California, Davis, offers a B.A. in English with writing emphasis and a one-year minimum (normally two-year) M.A. in Creative Writing.

Q: In your introduction to Calling the Wind, *you write that you tell your classes, first thing, "I think we can begin from the assumption that storytelling is vital to human health. It gives us workable metaphors for our lives." What do you mean by that, and what are some of those metaphors storytelling offers?*

Any good piece of fiction seems to me to come out of a place in the writer that is true—to put it very simply—a place that is true to who he or she is in terms of just basic human experience, the whole inner landscape of a human being. And at the same time, as I hear myself say this, I am thinking that this in itself is the most difficult thing for a writer to achieve—to stay in touch with the truth of who you are. Because that truth is always changing. The challenge for the writer, it seems to me, is to keep up with that changing truth, and to know how to identify it. It's a big, big task to ask any human being to have that kind of sensitivity every day in the week, to have that kind of command of him or herself.

Q: For young writers, would-be writers, I would think it would be especially difficult.

Absolutely. This is what I'm always trying to get my writing students to understand, because, although we all want to stretch out and try things slightly beyond our experience, to break new ground and reach into other territory in terms of the kind of subject matters we choose, it's a tricky business. It can be done, but it has to be done while at the same time staying in touch with all the really nebulous business going on inside that has a life of its own, that really knows more than the writer knows about what people are going to respond to.

Which is a long way of coming around to responding to your question. What people are going to respond to *is* that human element, and the writer has to stay in touch with that and it has to be true. The reader can tell instantly when it's not true.

Q: When the writer drifts too far from his inner truth, you mean.

Even if it's not the *reader's* truth. Or let me put it another way: Even if it doesn't have the same cultural definition as the reader's definition, the reader will still recognize the essential human truth of it.

Q: To what extent, then, should the writer be active in trying to create those metaphors, those truths, for someone other than himself? Or should he not try at all? In what sense should he be actively reaching outside himself?

That's a good question. I think it's a tricky business to make any conscious effort in that direction. Because very often you step onto your own feet, you get in your own way. To make a conscious effort, I think, is very often problematic.

You manage to do your best work, I believe, when you let it happen. When you find a way to listen to yourself, to let that true self give expression to itself. But let me just footnote that. You *do* have to make an early conscious effort at the same time in order to get to that truth. There is *always* the engagement of consciousness. It's just like dancing or skating or riding a bicycle. You learn how to ride a bicycle, to keep the two wheels going—but then you need to let it happen in a natural way. That may not be the best metaphor I can come up with, but I think it pretty much says what the creative process needs. It needs spontaneity and naturalness. If you're dancing, for example, and you're self-conscious and looking at your feet, you're going to lose your rhythm and get out of step.

Q: You've spoken of how much students from all backgrounds responded to the short stories by African-American writers that you've read to your classes, even though they previously hadn't heard of anyone aside from Richard Wright, James Baldwin, and Alice Walker. Why haven't those stories been used more?

Well, of course, we know why. We know of the whole perva-
sive existence of institutionalized racism, certainly in the curriculum, and the curriculum reflects the society. I think that
probably explains a great deal of it. There have been efforts on
the part of individual teachers to correct this and turn it around.
I think it's very refreshing to watch my students discover characters who happen to be African-American and be able to identify with them. It creates an enormous amount of excitement in
these kids to be able to see their own parents and themselves in
these characters.

Q: You even mentioned it transcended ethnic boundaries.

It's just amazing. You see the papers they write. They get
really turned on by that human element and identify totally.
They also realize that, once they get through the cultural trappings, human beings are all pretty much alike and have the
same kinds of aspirations and fears. It really makes a difference.

*Q: This goes back to what you were saying in the beginning. In
what sense should a writer who is trying to express a background,
a culture, an upbringing, bring that background to the fore, and in
what sense actively aim beyond it to universal concerns? It must
be an extremely difficult balance.*

And I'll tell you why. The necessary thing for any fiction
writer is to reach down deep enough in him or herself to connect with this magic that will make the writing talk to readers.
It's never a matter of getting *beyond* the ethnicity. I think it's a
matter of reaching deep enough into it, below it. In other words,
I like to think in vertical rather than horizontal terms—reaching
down to a subtextual level, below the purely social level of experience and staying in touch with that as one creates a piece of
fiction. I don't think it's any more difficult for the ethnic writer,
black or Chinese-American or whatever, because that task alone

is a very difficult thing for any writer to do. The tendency, no matter how smart or sensitive you are, is simply to reach for the easy identifying marks on the surface.

What you do, when you create a piece of fiction, is present a terrain that is essentially a surface. What makes it valuable to a reader, what makes it last as art, is the fact that a lot is going on beneath it, through implication. Teachers call it subtextual. All of it is implied. Hemingway had a term for it, the iceberg, the iceberg effect, where you show the tip and imply the rest. There's this huge, enormous amount below. The surface has to shimmer or vibrate in such a way as to radiate all of that other stuff beneath.

And it's pretty much the same for any writer. Life itself is enormously complex for anybody, and the business of trying to render it is always very tricky. I don't think any writer, no matter how intelligent, has any guarantee of being able to do this each time. I think you might succeed this year and then have a hell of time to repeat the performance. And you wouldn't even want to repeat it. To succeed you need it to be different.

Q: Those you've spoken of in the past who succeed at both levels, the surface experience and what's below—Ralph Ellison, Toni Morrison—do it so easily, effortlessly.

That's the magic of it. They've worked so hard it seems easy.

Q: But for a young student the stumbling blocks must be many in that regard.

The younger the writer, the more likely it is that he or she will not have had the experience to write about. There is also the possible problem of not being fully in command of the craft. Even if they feel things deeply, and many of them do—after age eighteen most people have enough experience to write a novel—the problem is to have distance as well as the technical ability to realize it.

Q: This might bring up the question of how one measures success in the classroom, both yours as a teacher and theirs as students. How would you define it?

Well, there are different kinds of success. In an undergraduate class, what I try to do is work with students on an individual level as much as possible, trying to create a context or atmosphere in which each student can discover what he or she needs to improve. Now, some people will come into an undergraduate workshop with more talent, some with less, and some will never be writers. No one is working at exactly the same level. In those cases where I know the student will never be a writer, I try to encourage that student to understand what makes the writing good, and through that help make them better readers. That's something that may stay with them the rest of their lives. With the others who are committed to writing and have talent, the only thing you can really do is be there for them and help them straighten out a few technical things, keep them on the right track. And that's what I do.

Now, in the graduate fiction workshop, it's much more likely that the participants will all be on a fairly advanced level. So you're talking to a different crowd. What I try to do there is treat them with respect, respect their talent, and talk with them pretty much as an editor would to a writer, to put it one way. To show them how to improve their work on technical terms and help them if there is some sort of conceptual problem.

Q: Are you trying to discover what they *are trying to do and help them with that?*

Yes, exactly, that's the main thing. And on the individual level, I tell my students all the time: Listen, you'll hear a lot of things in the workshop that are not going to be useful, and what I would advise you to do is be patient, sit through it, until you do hear something that is going to click with you. You are the only person who ultimately knows. You may not know it consciously yet, but eventually you will know what you need to do to make this thing work. Occasionally someone will say, "Well, how will I *know* when I hear what's right for me?" Well, you may not know what's right for you at the particular moment. I mean, that's one of the other things, at the risk of sounding immodest, that the instructor is there for, to sort of nudge the writers along in the right direction. Not to say, "Listen to this; don't listen to that," but to say, "Try this and see if it works." I try to be as diplomatic as I possibly can. I've discovered that a lot of good writers can be bad critics. But I don't want to alienate anyone. I'm not a rude person anyway. It's really a difficult tightrope to walk, to keep everybody on the positive side and also direct them where I think they're going to benefit from what they're exposed to.

Q: Even though you don't try to impose your own style, can it ever be a completely communal experience? You are the teacher, and maybe there are some implicit psychological effects of your presence there as one who simply knows.

Yes, that's very true. When I don't know, I'm very honest about it, but most of the time I think I do know. I've been doing this for twenty-five years, I've read enough, I regularly review books for newspapers, and I'm always thinking about books and stories in critical terms, so I think I have some kind of expertise and some kind of right to say something about these matters.

But as much as I know, I don't know everything, and I don't think I'm always right. I also believe that there is no single correct way of reading a story or correcting a story. There are several possible ways to go. I've discovered that when there are problems in a piece of fiction there are several possible ways to fix those problems. Assuming that one individual has the answer creates the danger of falling into a very narrow path.

Q: From what you've said elsewhere about the process of your own writing, it sounds as if you allow the experience you want to write about to bubble up in its own time—two months, six months, a year—and the form you choose to write in will find itself also, poetry or prose. Is that right?

Yes, but the later truth is that a novel is a whole other ballgame. I can feel a novel, a *true* novel, that is—not a novel that didn't get written, and there are a lot of those, too!—but a true novel I can feel coming on like a storm. You can feel the atmospheric pressure like the weather, the whole shift in climate—I can feel it gestating. It's different with poetry. Poetry tends to come in shorter, quicker, faster doses, in shots, but then of course it may take a long time to work out.

Q: Can you, in so many words, tell your students, "Look, whatever confinements you find here, be sure to ignore them later on, because you have to find your own rhythm and pace?"

Absolutely. I believe that. When they sit down to the blank page, that's a whole different experience. Nothing I or anyone else has said is going to really save them or help them that much—unless they've already absorbed it and forgotten it. You know what I mean? If they've absorbed the best of what's said, put it in a useful place, and understood it at a gut level, then they don't need to think about it anymore. Again, it's just like riding that bicycle; you don't think about what makes you stay up on two wheels. Well, when you sit down to that blank page it's really the way it has to be. If you sit there with lots of critical information in the fore part of your mind, you couldn't get anything written. You can't remember anything that Professor Major said, or anybody said, that's going to help you.

Q: I'm curious about the twelve years you spent teaching at the University of Colorado in Boulder. While you were there you spent time on a Zuni reservation, didn't you?

I did a lot of research for a novel on Zuni. I used to go down to New Mexico and Arizona a lot, to the Navaho and Zuni reservations. Initially, I got interested in the Zunis because they were visited—I guess it was in the 1580s but I can't remember precisely—by a giant African. They had never seen anyone like that and they immediately made him into a god. And he stayed there and lived among the Zunis for many years. Well, as it turned out, by the time I got around to writing the novel about the Zunis, which is called *Painted Turtle*, he was left out entirely. He doesn't appear at all, not even mentioned. Once I learned about modern-day Zunis—met some of them, got invited to some of the ceremonies, and so on—I got more interested in writing about contemporary culture. The novel is set in the 1960s and deals with a young Zuni woman who is raped. She gives birth to twins, which is a very magical but also a very troublesome and problematic thing for the Zunis, as it is for most tribal people. No one seems to know what to do about twins. It's some kind of blessing and curse at the same time. I included a lot of the ritual and ceremony and songs. She's a folk-song writer and guitar player who makes the circuit around to these cantinas, playing music. It's one of the books I'm proudest of. I feel close to that book. And though it's set in another culture, a culture I had to acquire, I felt that every moment of it came from the truest place in myself that I could conjure up. Which is another way of saying that, no matter what the cultural trappings are, or what the window dressing might be, or what the cultural decorations consist of, it's still necessary to tap into that level of human experience people will respond to.

Q: How limiting is it that students in a graduate writing workshop don't have the luxury of that kind of research and the time to throw out a character and pick one up?

Well, actually, that's not always true. One of my students last year, for example, a woman of Anglo-Saxon heritage, actually finished a novel about a young black girl based on her experience in Philadelphia. She became so involved with this girl's life she actually identified enough with her to be able to write a novel. It was a most convincing thing. You wouldn't believe as you picked it up that someone who wasn't black wrote it. That happens all the time and we don't notice it.

Richard Price, for example, did it just last year with *Clockers*, about a young drug dealer. And it's a genuine thing, a piece of art. He managed to get down to that genuine level that counts, rendering this drug deal in the most human, believable terms imaginable. So I take the position that the cultural stuff is fairly superficial; all you can do is understand what it means. The stuff that truly counts is beneath it. I could think of dozens of examples of that happening. For instance, James Baldwin writing *Giovanni's Room* with depth and sensitivity, which has no black characters in it whatsoever. And Richard Wright's *Savage Holiday*, with no black characters, and it's a truly felt, deeply rendered story. There are dozens and dozens of examples, and not just across racial lines but in many, many different cultures.

Q: James Joyce writing as Molly Bloom at the end of Ulysses?

That's another example. The whole false argument that you can't write as the other gender. It's ridiculous, and we have some of the best examples in the world to prove it. An equally good one is [Defoe's] *Moll Flanders* in the voice of a woman, one of the most believable female characters I've encountered, written by a man.

Q: Does this relate to what you have said about there being no single "black experience"—that it's rather many different individual experiences and thus available to a variety of people.

This is something Ralph Ellison wrote about in the introduction to the new edition of *Invisible Man*. He talks about how his experience growing up in the Southwest was a black experience but a particular kind of black experience that was very different from the particular black experience Richard Wright had in the Southeast. Both experiences might be culturally defined as "black," as African-American, but they're different. They're shaped by different geographical and historical forces, and these two men coming in contact with each other would have had some communication problems.

Q: So if Richard Price is successful, then, he is not trying to represent an ethnic experience as a whole but rather one individual character within that experience.

And that character has larger implications for a whole part of the culture, but can't be said to speak for the whole culture—just as we wouldn't expect Richard Nixon to represent all of Anglo-American culture.

Q: Let me just ask you: "A shimmer of verbal energy made visible" is your wonderful phrase about good language in fiction. How important do you find language for your students today; are they experimenting with it or is it incidental to the content they're looking for?

Most of my graduate writing students are operating on different levels. Some are more sensitive to language and care about the quality more than others, so it's difficult to generalize. I try constantly to talk about how important it is to have that sensitivity, not just to get a handle on the language but to get in touch with a kind of lyrical intensity that's necessary to make the reading experience truly vibrate, truly resonate, to give the reader the fullest advantage. Now, as I say that, I am also thinking that a lot of it simply has to do with talent, some innate individual talent.

Q: And you either have it or don't.

Yeah, I didn't want to say that, but that's what I was thinking.

Q: Is a talent for language, actually, the same as saying that someone understands the human voice, it's tone and rhythm?

I think so. That's what I mean. And some people have a sense of the voice, know how to listen and render that voice, just as some have a talent for music. Some have a good ear.

Q: I also wanted to ask you about the notion of a writing career. Rosellen Brown thought she remembered a quote from Toni Morrison to the effect that there was no such thing as a career in writing, that it really was just word after word, each individual effort one at a time. And then I ran across an article by James Fenton quoting Byron. Byron said that poetry is an expression of an excited passion, and that "there is no such thing as a life of passion any more than a continuous earthquake." And no such thing, therefore, as a life of poetry. Maybe that's what Toni Morrison was saying, too. What do you think?

I think they are both getting at the fact that it's never easy, that once you write a book, the experience of writing it will not in any way prepare you for the next one. It's always new, always fresh, always dangerous, always a struggle, word by word, step by step. And there are no guarantees. Unless of course you're writing formula fiction, where all twelve novels have this particular plot.

Q: Do you think students going into a program expect of that career a series of successful novels? Or do they see it as the struggle you described?

It looks very glamorous to them early on, a very glamorous way to live, to create these beautiful things called novels or poetry. I think at some point, if they're lucky, if they're smart enough, they realize it's a lot of hard work with uncertain benefits, a very risky business, and certainly not anything to go into expecting to make a lot of money. I think the ones who *have* to write will pretty much hang in there, because they're driven to do it.

Now, the tricky thing is that some people are driven to write even if they have no talent for writing. That's true. The two things have nothing or little to do with each other. Some people are driven to write who also have enormous amounts of talent and that's pretty lucky for them. But it still doesn't guarantee anything.

Q: And American writing programs, in that sense, are no different than anything else in life, I suppose. No guarantees. Although you've heard the criticism of them.

In twenty years we've seen our best writers come out of programs. I would say most of the best writers we have on the scene today—writers under forty—have come out of creative writing programs and have not been hurt by them—and some have even gained quite a bit.

The criticism that they all write alike is absurd; it's a prejudice with no truth whatsoever. It's a charge that's constantly made in print—I see it all the time—and it's absurd. We could create a list if we had the time of at least a dozen writers under forty who have come out of one program or another, and we could see just how different they are.

Q: Where did you learn to write, and from whom?

I never took any creative writing classes. I wish I had. I probably would have moved along faster than I did. It took a long time to evolve to a place where I could do good work. Had workshops been common, which they weren't. . . . Of course, in the context in which I grew up I can't say I regret that; they just weren't available. Very few people of my generation actually had workshop experiences. There were a few places I could have gone. Iowa was there, and Wallace Stegner was doing something at Stanford. But I can't think of other places actually involved in the teaching of creative writing in the sixties.

Q: But here you are, writing, teaching. . . . So how much would you say it hurt you that you didn't take these classes?

I think that had I the opportunity of insistent and continuous critical feedback, I would have benefited greatly. I didn't have people around me who could read my work and give me some smart criticism. I only had honest friends whose judgment I trusted. That was the way it was done.

Q: Do you feel you missed having role models in the classroom?

My role models were writers, I read their books, and I very often learned a lot from just the examples of the books. I can think of being absolutely swept away by one writer after another from the age of fifteen through twenty-one, being passionately devoted to them for that period of time. I think I learned a lot that way. I outgrew some of these obsessions, but I went through them and they were good for me. I was imitating these writers and that's a way of learning. It was a kind of apprentice-ship for me. So I found my way by reading and imitating.

Q: What about incorporating outside reading into your work-shops?

At the graduate level I don't use any texts, but at the under-graduate level I've used books and collections of stories. I think that's a good thing for writers beginning to get their feet wet, beginning to understand how to put words on the page that cre-ate a world we call fiction. I think it's really good at that level.

Q: Are your students clearly taken with certain fiction writers as models?

Oh yeah, absolutely. Not just [Raymond] Carver, but I have a student who is passionately devoted to a particular writer, and you can see it reflected in the work. There's nothing you can do about that but watch the student and help him or her in the technical things. In other words, when the echoes are strong, you know that it's just a phase and it's going to pass as the young writer gravitates to his or her own voice. And when they get through it they will retain some useful part of that experience, carrying it over into a fuller sense of self that has to be in place, out of which they write the real stuff.

Q: "Very few of us," you've written, "come to a piece of writing with the intention of giving it a chance to talk to us; we would rather talk to it." Do you feel even today, as an accomplished writer, that you should keep open to another book's influence?

Far less today for me. Although I will admit that there is that possibility. The tendency is still there—I won't deny it—that if you read something you really like, you can actually absorb something and find yourself echoing it.

Yes, the tendency is there and we're open to it. That's why we read, isn't it? If not to have our lives changed, certainly to enlarge and deepen our sense of what our experience is all about.

Eve Shelnutt

(PHOTOGRAPH BY GREG SHELNUTT)

Born in Spartanburg, South Carolina, Eve Shelnutt won the *Mademoiselle* Fiction Award for the first story she wrote in her first creative writing class. The recipient of O. Henry and Pushcart Prizes, among others, Shelnutt has written three collections of short fiction (including *The Musician*, 1987) and three of poetry (most recently *First a Long Hesitation*, 1991); she is also author or editor of several highly acclaimed books on the creative writing process, among them *The Writing Room: Keys to the Craft of Fiction and Poetry* (1989) and *Writing, the Translation of Memory* (1990).

Eve Shelnutt received her M.F.A. in 1973 from the University of North Carolina at Greensboro, under the tutelage of Fred Chappell. She has become, over the course of nineteen years teaching both undergraduate and graduate creative writing at institutions like the University of Pittsburgh and Ohio University, a compelling voice in the analysis of American writing programs. A passionate defender of the value of intellectual development, she has written that writing programs need to produce not "more writers" but "*better* writers for whom the latest fads in fiction and poetry need to be questioned...I'm trying to help [my students] understand the relationship between art and contemplation, art and questioning, art and irony, in its deepest sense."

In these pages she explains why she has replaced the ever-present workshop class with a rigorous, analytical method of her own design. This conversation followed an undergraduate intermediate fiction class I witnessed at Ohio University during Fall 1992, where this new method was applied with apparent success; her students seemed impressively lively and interested, with high output in both their fiction and critical essays. Shelnutt has recently begun testing her non-workshop method at the graduate level as well.

Ohio University, in Athens, Ohio, offers a B.A. in English with a concentration in Creative Writing, an M.A. in English with creative thesis, and a Ph.D. in English with creative dissertation.

Q: You've been outspoken in your criticism of American creative writing programs and the workshops that are typically run in them. First of all, what do you see as some of the problems with these programs—and their causes?

The first problem, as I see it, is that creative writing as a discipline had a difficult time being accepted in the university.

It was a new discipline, coming into being rather late, fifty or so years ago at the University of Iowa and disseminating from there. Since creative writing teachers from the start had to fight for a place in academe, their posture was often aggressive or defensive. That was probably understandable; on the other hand it seemed to be self-perpetuating. Writing faculty found themselves—often due to their own efforts—very much apart from English departments as a whole. Creative writing became a process that was seen as difficult to understand, rather than as it truly was, simply intellectual work under a kind of apprenticeship-in-the-arts program. Too, writing programs didn't take well enough into account the great cultural changes that were happening in the world: television, for instance. And finally, when writing programs were asked to document themselves in terms of their validity and what constitutes success, their faculty turned to touting the publication of their students: "Yes, we are successful because our students publish."

Many cultural symptoms collided—unanticipated, unintended—to make creative writing a discipline that was growing its own unexamined problems, but I think the result of all this was that publication became almost an end in itself. Then, with what is called the "renaissance" of American fiction post-1970, the publishing industry began to see, with minimalism in particular, a way to package American fiction almost the way New Journalism was being packaged: writing that talks about the way we live now, writing that appeals to a reader who spends a lot of time in front of the television. In the eighteen years I've been a part of the profession, students are less well read and

195

much hungrier to publish quickly. Youth is touted in anthologies such as the *Twenty Under Thirty* volume; publishers seem to want to tout the *lives* of young writers as much as the work—and it helps if they are young and attractive and their pictures can be put on the backs of books. This all seeped down as information to young writers, who were increasingly entering these writing programs. I think all of this has not been beneficial to contemporary American literature nor necessarily to the reputation of writing programs.

Q: And what is the result, as you see it? Are students underprepared to write well, or do they write within too narrow a frame?

Well, I think they write *adroitly*. Given the competition to get into graduate writing programs, the students we see are adroit writers.

Q: John Gardner once said, "On a technical level at least, writing has never been better off."

Yes, yes. I think there's an analogy with sports. The better training and equipment, the more records get broken. At the level of imitative style, the expertise is surely high, but I'm not certain it makes for a literature with a great deal of depth, complexity, or that even serves the writers themselves well. That is to say, I'm not certain that our programs are asking young writers, in relation to world literature: "What is your vision as a writer over a *long period of time*?" We rather seem to be more product-oriented than oriented toward imagining a student's forty- or fifty-year career and preparing him or her for that long haul.

No, I don't think they're prepared, and what it means, finally, is that we are letting students go through our writing programs, particularly at the undergraduate level, without our seriously engaging them as future *artists*. They often take creative writing courses as just another course. To me, creative writing is not just another course. It is a *profound* question that's being asked,

often within a very short period of time. Society does not necessarily invite people to become writers, no more than it asks
them to become any other kind of artist. I feel that I have to
have students understand the *questions* that art poses to them,
in terms of a way to live, a focus of their minds in study, and the
rewards that it can contain.

*Q: In your essay "Notes from a Cell: Creative Writing Programs in
Isolation," [in* Creative Writing in America, *1989] you say that
writers ask, "What are the* stars *doing?" not "What do I want to
write?"*

Yes, the stories about Jay McInerney, Tama Janowitz, Bret
Easton Ellis, Amy Tan, etc., have given students the notion that
there is a career to be made in writing. It's not a bad notion. But
that career seems to be defined more by notions of fame and
notoriety and making a big splash than as a profession in the
way that Katherine Anne Porter talks about it in her *Paris
Review* interview. You know from her work that she means profession in a sense quite different from that understood by many
students today.

I remember in particular passing through a university where
students had a chance to suggest a visiting writer for a semester
in their program. They were choosing a writer whose work they
didn't know and about which they didn't particularly care, but
that writer had "made it" very quickly and they wanted to learn
what connections he had and if he could help them "connect." It
was very distressing to me to hear students talk that way. Now, I
think the state of the economy, which makes everyone panicked, influences us a great deal, but I'm not sure that in writing
programs we do much to deflect the pressure from the economy and the mass media on students.

*Q: There was a student at the Hollins College program, which I
visited, who spoke highly of the unpressured atmosphere there, of
using his time there as time off from marketplace pressures.*

There are several programs which have that sort of reputation. Hollins has long been one of them. The University of North Carolina at Greensboro, where I studied, is another. It's the place where Randall Jarrell taught, Alan Tate visited the program, George Garrett. . . . But it's Fred Chappell who has been the dominant presence in that program for twenty years, and his idea of the writer's craft, the writer's life, the writer's depth of seriousness, has made a good program. I have a graduate student there right now. I think it's the best place he could have chosen.

Q: So your criticism is by and large focused more toward programs where the competitive edge seems to be more quickly honed?

Yes; it isn't that I don't think writing is finally competitive. How we define competition in writing, however, is crucial. I tell my students they'll be judged, finally, long after they're dead, against *world* literature. It's one of the reasons I don't have a workshop in my classes. Students often get the idea in workshops that they're competing with one another, but in fact the rate at which one student develops is quite different from that of any other. The notion that the students are competing with one another in a workshop is a narrow view. I think the *nonworkshop* format lets students know that their competition is not there, that in fact it's a much broader world of competition—that they can only try to write well enough to have their work survive, and that even to ask the right questions about how one might write that well is extremely difficult. But certainly the standards will be world standards and not in relation to any other ten or twelve people in a workshop.

Q: Now, before asking you to outline your nonworkshop approach, let me ask you flat out: How much of your overall view is a matter of taste, personal taste? Your interest in world literature, for instance—you often speak of Nadine Gordimer, V. S. Naipaul, Milan Kundera. Do you think these writers bring something to literature that others don't?

Well, there's no doubt that my aesthetics have a great deal to do with what I say and do as a teacher and how I organize my classes. I tell my students that writing teachers are not inter-changeable, that they *have* a point of view. We have students going into our graduate program who have never read anything by the teachers they're going to study with, and I tell them that that's not self-protective, it's not wise. I admit at the beginning of every course I teach that I *am* teaching with a point of view, that I'll make my aesthetics known to them, and that I hope my aesthetics, as well as theirs, will be up for discussion and argument.

On the other hand, it seems to me that one of the problems any writer faces is being locked into his or her culture. At the simple level of logic I have said to myself as a writer, and I say it to my students: Since we are surrounded by American culture, including its writing, we must ask ourselves questions about how that culture has influenced us and how we can get a perspective that *questions* that culture. I myself feel locked within a culture that I question all the time, one that has shaped my vision of writing. It's one of the reasons I've asked my students not to be disdainful of contemporary criticism, which they have a tendency to be because the language disturbs them in its difficulty.

Q: But some people—Madison Smartt Bell, for one—although they agree with the questions and problems you raise, don't agree that the marriage of the writing program and the English department's emphasis on critical theory is necessarily the best answer for creative writers.

I think there are certain myths that writers have fostered and used self-protectively but not necessarily wisely. One of them has been the notion of the artist as possessing a fragile creativity, easily damaged—as if the language of contemporary critical theory would somehow ruin the mind or ruin the sense of language the writer has, that knowing it can destroy a kind of unconscious creativity. This has been a notion that writers have enjoyed and, I think, misused. *My* notion, as I tell my students, is that, whatever the creative urge is, it can only be *strengthened* by questions and all manner of texts; that it is *not* fragile; indeed, that it is bottomless. And that to turn away from new ideas on the basis of protecting a cupful of creativity that can dry up in the least amount of sunlight is a self-defeating way to think about what we call creativity.

That's not to say that all creative writers need to use the language of poststructuralist critical theory. But students certainly need to be conversant with some of its major themes and be able to accept that it's out there. I think I say in that essay, "Notes from a Cell," that to ignore and to be disdainful and aggressive against those theories is akin to acting as if abstract painting had never existed, or as if we had no music prior to Schoenberg. We would never in music or art take the positions we as writers take against critical theory.

Q: I see that in the syllabus to your introductory class you've written, "I have devised a course that mirrors more directly my understanding of how writers develop. Artistic showmanship will be deemphasized and individual intellectual development will be emphasized. This realistically mirrors a writer's position outside of workshops." Since workshops are used almost everywhere, describe if you would the class method I saw practiced last night, and your reasons behind its changes.

It's true, students expect workshops. There's also an efficiency about them in terms of time: Stories are discussed by ten or twelve people, with or without a teacher's written comment, and the major work is done during the class meeting. However, I began to question the method when I saw that students were writing to please one another and to please me publically. I also recognized and was somewhat appalled by the fact that we have students entering undergraduate and graduate programs who have not read much at all. For several years I was shocked at that, because, coming out of a reading family and background, I always assumed that writers naturally consumed books all the time; but in fact that's not the case.

So I began slowly to turn my focus on the study of literature as creative writers would study literature, for insights into form, into strategies, into what makes one piece of writing not simply a reiteration but in fact a creation: what makes Kafka *Kafka*. I began to focus more on *reading*.

And with that I decided that my students should not be in a workshop at all, that they should not see one another's work, that only I would see their work. One of the unfortunate aspects of the workshop as I experienced it was that students began to treat the teacher simply as one more voice in the room. Well, I'm *not* simply one more voice in the room. I openly declared that I am able to read students' work with some objectivity and a legitimacy in regards to their development, that I do not seek to have students mirror my style, and that I am serving their best interests. And, you see, when I alone comment on their stories, I can pressure my students to work harder than they can be pressured to work within a discussion format.

So, although students do write three or four full-length stories a semester (and by full-length I mean twelve to sixteen double-spaced typed pages), I decided that I wanted class time taken up with discussion of published texts and of form and language. I assign two stories a week for them to read and two formal essays a week for students to write—twenty-two essays a semester. I put emphasis on the word "formal" because I don't just want opinion pieces, I want third-person studies of the stories' formal properties. My students are marked present *only* when they come to class with those essays. Since they have worked long and hard and read the stories two or three times in order to write the essays, they come to class with something they want to say, a perspective they want to defend.

Thus, as you've seen, class consists of very lively arguments between students about form, theme, various devices. It also allows me a place to make comments about strategies writers might use, suggestions they might follow, without fear of damaging an ego. And since my students are quite rewarded by the process in class, they do trust me to comment on their own creative work.

Q: And your students don't read each other's stories. That's different, too.

It's not that several of the students don't get together and share their work outside of class. That's fine. But in class they only see each other's creative work during the last meeting. We use a printing service; they choose their best formal essay and best story, which is itself a very interesting process for them—they have to decide on what basis they're making their choice and what they want to present to others. And then we go as a group and purchase the packets. It's wonderful to see students sitting around silently for an hour or so avidly reading each other's work. Then they take the booklet home and I'm sure read every word.

I should mention that at Ohio University we have evaluations every single quarter in every single class: I have a great deal of documentation that students much prefer this method to the workshop method. They write at great lengths about what it gives them. And I've had several other people test this method on the undergraduates. It was important to me that I not think that the success of the method only issued from my personality but that the method works regardless of who uses it. There are particular things that I am able to give in class discussion, but other teachers give other things. At any rate, I now have genuine data on the method—it took me a long time to get it, and it underscores the viability of the method: Students' stories are *much* stronger for its use.

Q: Last night in class, as you handed back a story, you said to one of your students, "Change the perspective of the next story, change the number of characters, create a new depth of subtlety."

Well, you see, one of the focuses of my classes is to have my students perpetually push against their limitations, even to have them push against what they do best. Because the natural tendency is to win the game, that is, to repeat what one has succeeded at. And I say to my students that this is a danger, that you have to be careful even of your gifts because you can find yourself in a trap. You must perpetually work at expanding your range of devices and of vision of form, because you *will* one day hit forty or fifty, you will have written a huge amount by that time, and that's when writing finally gets the most interesting. What do you do when you have done everything that comes "naturally"? It's really more exciting *after* that point. You hit various walls as a writer when you're clearly tested, and I try to give students a sense of what they'll be up against later. In general, I think writers have not been particularly self-protective against the kind of praise heaped on style. Conrad was, but Hemingway and Ray Carver I don't think were. The reviewing press is not meant to be the watchdog of writers' aesthetic development or their whole careers. So when I find a student repeating him or herself stylistically or thematically or using devices over and over again, I say, "Fine, what else do you know?"

Q: Your courses change from the beginning undergraduates, who receive a stricter program, to the more advanced ones, don't they?

Yes, in the first course that students take at the undergraduate level, I must do a lot of talking about form itself. What is a scene? How does time pass in a short story? We go over point of view again and again and again. By the time these students have reached the intermediate level they rarely make point-of-view transgressions. I'm working more on subtlety at that point, on fluidity, complexity, and density of language.

Q: It sounds as if you're trying to prepare them in a way you believe every undergraduate student should have been prepared in the first place. Making up for a lack of education?

Well, of course I *would* say that. The students in the under-graduate program here that I send on to the graduate programs have a vocabulary about which to speak of stories, should they find themselves in a workshop setting. That is to say, they know the language, they know the terms, they know the names for the shapes of stories. It's work done from the beginning of the introductory course, and as you saw last night, students use this vocabulary very confidently.

Q: "Metaphorical constructs," "historical antecedents," "the absurdist tradition." Most of them seemed comfortable and engaged.

And in their formal essays they must talk about scenes, how many, how time passes, how the formal properties are arranged, etc. And so, students that enter from my undergraduate classes into a graduate program would, first, have a critical language.

Second, they would have practice discussing and writing about stories by professional writers. In the beginning classes we study one writer's work, a collection of stories, whether it's Gina Berriault's *The Infinite Passion of Expectation* or *On the Island* by Josephine Jacobsen; I've used Paul Bowles's collected stories and the collected stories of Katherine Anne Porter, and so on—and they are able to compare and contrast stories. As you saw, when they compare stories from *The Art of the Tale* text I use at the intermediate level they have a sense how form itself plays a part in the writer's developing conception of fiction. I think it's an important step.

Third, they also develop a high critical standard. Not only do I ask them to choose *their* best stories for the anthology we put together for their work, but I also often start discussions by asking them if they can decide which story—of two I want them to compare by professional writers—has the greater weight. And we talk about why we have chosen one story over another and students have to make a case for which they weigh as aesthetically more sound, more enduring, more compelling in a number of ways.

And fourth, I have them edit. They must write essays without errors in punctuation, grammar, or spelling; they must shape the formal essays logically, documenting what they say in MLA style by using quotations from the text. So they're learning skills as well as an art form. The students I send on to other teachers and through the graduation process *can* write formal essays. If these students do enter a workshop, they will be very well prepared.

Q: Let me go back to your second point, the assigning of required texts to read. Wallace Stegner [in On the Teaching of Creative Writing*] has said, "A writer is a whole individual, stealing from whoever can help him, and ranging all of life and literature for his clues. Assigning him set readings would be like sending a young Dali . . . to copy the 'Mona Lisa.' It would be a way to make academic writers, not good ones."*

Well, Wallace Stegner started teaching some time ago. He entered at a time when he could probably count on the writers who studied with him being inherently good readers. If I thought that every fledgling writer who came into my class was an avid reader, devouring books, then my teaching would be quite different. But my students have read very little on their own.

Many writers choose to write without having done the necessary preparation, and that is: to become readers. There is a kind of arrogance we have given young writers that lets them assume that ignorance is not something to be critical of. They tend to be very self-accepting, and I spend a lot of time disabusing them of their infinite confidence in themselves as writers so long as they're unprepared to be writers. I tell them that I am against the idea of writers as primitives, intellectually. Nadine Gordimer they find particularly difficult—and sometimes they can feel very aggressive against her work. I tell them that struggle with a text is not a negative; it can be one of its rewards.

Q: And you're about to try your methods on graduate students, aren't you? That would have to be a different thing entirely.

Yes, the question might occur, "How can you teach that way when you already have more sophisticated students? They're older, they've been through an undergraduate program, they've been chosen for a graduate program and vied for a fellowship?" To which I would reply, "I haven't found them a lot more sophisticated than many seniors I teach." They are to some extent better read, of course, but they aren't widely or deeply read, and they don't always have a good vocabulary by which to speak about stories. So I'll be very interested to see how it goes. I plan to follow much the same program. I've ordered very many more books for them to read, but they will also write the formal essays and discuss the stories, and I'll be the only one to read their creative work, again in order to downplay the competition.

Q: You write of trying to create "lifetime readers and lifetime writers." In your essay "Undergraduate Writing Programs in the Nineties" [1992] you spoke of concerning yourself with the "character" of your students in a broad sense. What did you mean?

Yes. Students have very little contemplative time, very little peace and quiet. Television is partly to blame, immersing them in ways of thinking that would not create an artist of any sort. I suppose I'm trying to return students to the notion of contemplation, the value of interiority, the joy of being lost in reading, and the joy of having literature raise profound questions instead of answer contemporary problems. There's been far too much praise of contemporary literature as helping readers understand "how we live now." That's not what literature is finally for. Literature asks far more questions than it answers. I want students to return to the deep sources of their own personalities. Many students come to college, naturally, with a sense of first freedom, of having answers and wanting to use fiction as a soapbox or as expiation. All of that is a function of youth. But I don't think students are aware of the extent to which they have been influenced by a television-dominated culture. I'm trying to help them understand the relationship between art and contemplation, art and questioning, art and irony, in its deepest sense.

So I suppose a lot of my work, when I speak of working on the character of my students, is in helping them answer the question, "Why would anyone spend an entire lifetime producing art?" I don't think that they have posed the question themselves, and I think that if they are to have a chance at being writers they *must* pose that question and do so in short order. They must try to connect not only with the particular story they are writing at the moment but with the whole idea of what art does for humanity, and why one would give up a great deal of the rewards of a consumer society for the sake of art. These are questions I don't think society focuses on.

I experience a great deal of joy as a writer, which I would like for students to be able to envision as theirs, too. It takes a long time to develop enough skill to understand what that reward is. I try to give students a sense of how to get good enough to experience the reward—the kind of work they'll have to do to ask themselves the legitimate questions that art poses. But, in a way, my relationship with their developing characters is against an entire society not particularly interested in the artist.

You know, students aren't very happy with contemporary American society, but no one has told them it's OK to be unhappy with it. At a time when everyone thinks everyone is supposed to be happy, students are troubled. What they say to me is that they truly appreciate having their *highest* aspirations taken seriously. That's why they are so willing to work in my classes; I *do* treat them seriously. The lecture I give them on the first night of each class says that the work is not going to be easy. Only the hardy stay in the room and eventually they let me know that they appreciate work as a value. I pose no easy answers, but I do take their highest aspirations seriously. They know I'm going to chastise them for only wanting to write stories that other people have written or for not really wanting to work as writers. Finally, they appreciate that. I want the reputation I have, that my courses are going to be hard. I myself have yet to get over how hard it is to be a writer. There was a time when I thought, "It's got to be easier someday." But it's never easier. It's increasingly difficult. I know that I could not have taught the way I do now the first year out of graduate school, or the third or fifth. I didn't know enough about how hard it was going to be.

Now, there's a degree to which this *is* what Fred Chappell gave me in graduate school. In ways that I can't even describe, he stands there as an image of what an artist can be. I had been immersed in dead writers for so long, and there was someone of the same vision of art as Dostoevsky and Tolstoy and Chekhov, living, breathing, making a career himself. In a way, in a much different style, I'm trying to give that sense to my students. And what they say is that they appreciate it tremendously. That's the rewarding thing; that's the only thing that keeps me at it.

Jane Smiley

Born in Los Angeles in 1949, Jane Smiley attended Vassar College and the University of Iowa Writers' Workshop, where she received both an M.F.A. and Ph.D. Between "a competent murder mystery" called *Duplicate Keys*, her third novel, and *The Greenlanders*, her fourth, her writing underwent "a significant aesthetic sea change," she says here. What followed were the critically lauded novellas *The Age of Grief* (1987) and *Ordinary Love* and *Good Will* (1989), succeeded in turn by the novel *A Thousand Acres* (1992), for which she won the Pulitzer Prize for fiction.

As a teacher of creative writing at Iowa State University since 1981, Jane Smiley has devised an original, highly structured method that forswears critical praise of any kind for students' work. In so doing, she ushers writers away from the arena of criticism and into one of analysis. "The key is not thinking of student stories as 'good' and 'bad,'" she says in these pages, "but thinking of them as examples of some mode of analysis that can be used in an educating way." With insight into the process of creativity, her own and her students', she also speaks of the "rituals of evasion" that every writer develops. What emerges here is a serious, innovative blend of analysis, experience, and objective standards, all rendered into practical terms for the developing writer.

Jane Smiley's newest novel is *Moo*, to be published in Spring 1995.

Iowa State University, in Ames, Iowa, offers a B.A. in English and a two-year M.A. in English with Creative Writing emphasis.

Q: You've developed an analytic method of teaching creative writing at Iowa State that excludes praise of any kind. First of all, would you give me a little history—how did it develop?

Well, the graduate side of our program was very minimal until about 1984, when we decided to use some fellowships we had to lure better students. So by fall of 1984 we had a fairly decent group of graduate students, and they were in a class with a colleague of mine here, but almost all of them were men.

Q: By the luck of the draw?

Just by coincidence. And he had had some trouble with that class. They had problems with antagonism and rivalry that worked against any sort of coherent teaching method. I knew I was going to get all or most of the students the next semester and that there had been bad blood, so I thought, "What can I do to minimize the bad blood between the students and take the pressure off of me as a kind of judge and chooser between them?" One of the things that is true here, as well as elsewhere, is the wide difference between the amount of experience and talent of the class members. You'll have some very good students and some beginning students in the same class, and that can create a lot of friction in fiction.

Q: Fiction friction?

A lot of fiction friction, because obviously students are suspicious of what they are getting from one another. So I decided that the best thing to do, for a number of reasons, was come up with a structure that in some sense would be impersonal and would direct their attention away from me and each other and toward the ongoing progress of their work. To begin with, I divided them up into smaller groups of five, although I didn't dictate who would be in each group. Also, I had been thinking for quite a long time about a structure that would allow constant revision. Since we have a sixteen-week semester, including exam week, I decided each student would have to write four stories with four drafts per story. That meant that in each small group we would read everyone's draft for the week, and talk about them.

Q: So you had to put in a good deal more time.

Well, it requires about four and a half hours each week instead of three, since I meet with three groups of five for an hour and a half each. It *is* more time-consuming but it has a good payoff, so I'm not bothered.

Q: Do the students ever meet all together?

No, not after the first group. Once in a while they say, "Oh, gee, we'd like to," but what turns out to have happened is that the smaller groups have learned to speak a certain language among themselves, and they experience the other groups as a kind of intrusion. So even if they want to, it usually doesn't work. What they discover is that they've become quite intimate with their own group and they don't want to give up that intimacy.

Q: What happens during the course of a student's four drafts of each story?

Well, the first draft they turn in they're usually pretty proud of, and they think of it as fairly polished. And with the first story always, no matter how hard I've prepared them and no matter how hard they've tried not to, what they're really seeking is praise. They want for the impossible thing to happen, for me and the class to say, "This is great, you don't have to do any more drafts, just send it off now and it'll get published, I guarantee it." In my experience the first drafts are fairly short, fairly polished, and with some problem in them that seems fairly minimal. Let's say the section that's supposed to be the climax will be confusing. So we'll talk about that and we'll say that the person has to clear up the confusing parts of the climax for next week. But usually that involves all sorts of other things, too, like a more careful defining of the characters, or making the rising action move more slowly and clearly. It ends up requiring a kind of narrative restructuring just to make the climax less confusing.

As soon as they open up this box of the first draft, which is in, what shall we say, a state of *faux* completion, then the whole thing starts to fall apart. And the second draft is often a mess, because they are trying to bring in or explore elements that aren't in balance anymore. They're usually disappointed with the second draft; there's more to it but it's more of a mess, too. The third draft is better but still in a state of "uncontrol." But often by the time we've talked about the third draft we're all saying, "Aha!" and what we're saying "Aha" about is that we as readers feel that we finally understand what the author is getting at, and the author finally understands where *he's* going, too. Usually then they feel a certain amount of self-confidence about going on to the fourth draft, and it's really much better and more complete but often still unfinished. So they say they want to do a fifth draft, and I say, "No, you have to go on to the next story."

Q: Are you trying to get them to stay in the swim of the process of writing longer without having to produce a finished product?

Oh, absolutely. Ultimately, because they have to turn in a draft a week, they have to get in the habit of sticking with it, and the effect is that a lot of rituals have to be broken down. They resent that and resist it, because in my opinion rituals are a way of evading commitment to your work. When the rituals get broken down, they resist, because that means they can't evade it anymore. There's a whole separate subject I've thought a lot about, which is various types of evasion of commitment. This method is pretty good at breaking down those evasions, but it's not foolproof. We can go into that a little bit later.

Q: OK. For now, how about the progression, as you see it, of the four stories you get per person? Four is actually a pretty sizable number per semester.

Yeah, it is. Well, most of the stories, in a sort of bumbling and starting fashion, get better over the semester. At the same time the students go deeper and deeper into despair, because when you're doing four stories in sixteen weeks you kind of have your face pushed right into your characteristic problem. That problem keeps coming up and coming up, and it can lead to despair. But almost always the students solve some of the problems and so the despair they're feeling by the third story dissipates a little, because they see by the fourth story they've made a breakthrough.

Q: And you offer no praise at all?

Right. That was partly incidental because I had all these students who I knew would be seeking praise, since that had been their downfall the previous semester. And with the diversity of talent in the class, inevitably some people would get praise and some people wouldn't, and I wanted to keep them all on the right track and didn't want the ones who were less talented to feel alienated from the class. So I decided that I would try an analytical approach to their work.

Q: You never say, "Gee, I really liked this part of the story."

Never. I never say "like," I never say "don't like," never "good," never "bad." I say instead, "Why do you think so-and-so did this?" One of the things that I've discovered is that they get more interested in their own and each other's work when you start talking about artistic choices and stop talking about "good" and "bad," because they get interested in the system that's at work and they want to analyze that system. At first they're resentful of the fact that they aren't getting any praise, and often the most resentful ones were the most highly praised in the past; they perceive the absence of praise as a criticism. But I try to warn them, I try to tell them early on that they're going to have these feelings—but they're never going to know that I personally like their work or not.

Q: Isn't it difficult not to hint at an opinion? A raised eyebrow?

Not anymore. It was in the old days, but now it's automatic. You see, when you teach writing, you're teaching to students and beginners, and you owe it to them not to praise them. Well, *I* would say you owe it to them not to praise them; others would say you owe it to them not *simply* to praise them. Either way, with praise you are passing up an opportunity to help them see what the goal is, to intellectually see it and to instinctively perceive it.

Q: And you say the students eventually stop looking for that praise?

Right. Because they realize that if I give them praise it's a way of not engaging them with analysis. They come to see praise as a shortcut and they don't want it anymore. They find it unserious. They really do want to be taken seriously. At first they don't realize that's what they want. They think to be taken seriously is to be praised; but eventually they become convinced that to be taken seriously is to be analyzed and delved into. And so if I just say, "Gosh, this is good, I really like it," they'll wait and be upset if I don't go on.

Q: And what do you find comes out of that? It's almost a retooling of the way one thinks about the process of reward and punishment in one's work.

I think a number of things happen. One thing is everybody feels pretty much like an artist. Everybody feels like they're on an equal footing. And I think in some ways, though not all ways of course, they're on an equal footing with *me* because I'm no longer dishing out the rewards, I'm just asking the questions. They certainly feel like they're on an equal footing with one another.

Mostly, though, I think the best thing about it is that their work becomes more and more fluid. They don't have to protect or defend anything. What I always tell them is, "If I tell you that this paragraph or this sentence or this character is good, and then if you decide that the character has to be changed, you're going to be torn between your sense of the character and the praise you've received for it." I want the work to continue to be fluid until the writer says—or publication says—this is finished.

Q: Were there any teachers in your development who you liked very much and learned from?

No.

Q: None?

I had teachers that I liked personally, and I had teachers who liked my work, but part of the reason I developed this method was that I felt I didn't get effective teaching.

Q: So the next question of course is, what do you do in place of praise? How do you critique a story?

Well, the main problem with saying you're going to use an analytical method rather than a critical one is that you have to have a theory to back up the analytical method. Because of that, I've devised my own theory of how fiction works that I bring into the classroom and use as the basis for the analysis. It's fairly simple and easy to understand, but I think it works pretty well for beginning fiction writers. It's not all that sophisticated.

There used to be a book called *Writing Fiction*—there probably still is—by a man who taught at Brown named [R. V.] Cassill. I remember he spoke about five elements of fiction, but I lost the book so I had to come up with my own five. I decided the elements of fiction are: action, character, theme, setting, and language. In most short stories one or another of these elements predominates. And each predominating element has a particular payoff. For example, the payoff for action would be suspense; the payoff for setting would be a sense of the exotic. And if the writer has that as the main element but doesn't give that payoff, then the story fails at the bottommost level.

Q: The expectation must be met between reader and writer.

Right, right. That kind of analysis leads to the theory of the story as an exchange of expectations, or let's say a negotiation about expectations on the part of both the reader and the writer. The student writer's responsibility is not to fulfill the reader's expectations but to understand them, and to use that understanding to manipulate them. And there's a degree to which, if the writer wants to take something away from the reader, he must also give something back.

So for example: Most experimental fiction writers, like William Gass, took away from the reader a lot of things, such as belief in character, belief in suspenseful action. The thing they had to give back to the reader, since they were relying almost completely on theme, was a real sense of learning something, a real sense of enlightenment. If they fail to say something intellectually new or complex, the reader feels that that piece of experimental fiction has failed in some essential way.

Another example would be a writer of comic fiction. Now, comic fiction relies very profoundly on language rather than anything else. That means when the language fails, even if the characters are good and the action is interesting, the reader feels that the promise of this being comic or funny all the way through is broken, so it fails as a piece of comic fiction.

We talk about those things. We talk about plotting, we talk about character transformation, we talk about willing suspension of disbelief. We talk about things that are very basic, but we talk about them as an exchange: How do you get your reader to invest in this piece of fiction, and once the reader has made his investment, how do you not jeopardize it, or, if you're going to jeopardize it, how do you regain it?

Q: And it's these five elements that provide you with the tools of conversation in the class?

Right. It takes them a while to learn the language but pretty soon they learn that, too.

Q: How would you analyze a Raymond Carver story, say, using your five elements? Which of the elements predominates?

Oh, I would say probably a combination of character and theme. Language and setting are important, but if we weren't drawn into a deep sympathy with the characters, the individual stories might fail.

I guess I came up with this method because I'm not a judgmental person. It's not that I consciously don't like it, it's that I don't have a habit of mind of doing it. Having an analytical structure is a protection for the student as well as a way for him to learn about his own work. Where every student eventually arrives is a place where the formal problems of the work are the same as the psychological problems of the student and the philosophical problems of the student's worldview. And that's a good place for students to arrive; it also shows that the formal problems of the work are now deeper.

Let's say you have a student whose fictional characters are wafty and undefined. After you've had that student for a while you realize that *that's* the student, *that* is his or her problem. Every teacher, I think, has an instinctive perception that the problems in a student's work are in some sense beyond the teacher, that they are rooted in the student. But if you give that student an analytical framework and an understanding of the formal elements of fiction, while you may never solve the student's psychological problems, you may give them a way to attack the formal problems and come to an imaginative understanding of them. Do you see what I mean?

Q: I think so—and you yourself as a teacher don't involve yourself with the psychological elements.

No. See, I keep that to myself. If I come to see a student in a certain way and come to see the link between what's going on in his work and his life, I never say anything. I think that's intrusive. But I might become focused on what you could call the formal dilemmas of the work, and then we can talk about them as if they were purely formal dilemmas. Maybe the student will never solve these things in his life, but he may be able to address these formal dilemmas in his fiction.

Q: Tell me, do you use this method in your undergraduate as well as graduate courses?

Well, not so much with the undergraduates, because they aren't as dedicated to writing fiction. What they need more is to develop their imaginations, and so what I do in class is to give them a number of types of assignments that will let them think about different subjects in different ways.

Q: One question people might have is how easy it was for you to learn to teach this way—and how easy, or difficult, it might be for others to learn your method.

Sometimes I think you have to have a knack for getting the students not to focus on you, not to write stories *to* you, not to try to please you. And I don't know if I even have that knack as much as I'd like.

Q: In some classes for some teachers, of course, being on stage is part of their method.

Well, the last thing I would want to be is charismatic, a charismatic teacher. I almost think it's better to play away from any imputation of that, to downplay it, to be more self-effacing than you even want to be.

It *is* comfortable for me to do it this way, but after all I took it from Cassill. And so I think people who weren't me could learn to do it this way, too. Of course the method would change as they did it, but I think they could learn to be structure oriented and analytical and uncritical, and they could learn to reward the students, in a sense, for following their own desires.

I mean, in order for the students to get any benefit from following their own desires, they need to understand what a competent story is, what the mainstream, well-written story is. If you didn't believe as a teacher that there were any objective standards, then you couldn't teach the students the way I teach them. You wouldn't be able to raise them above a certain level of competence and then rely on them to bring their own ideas and personalities into the culture.

To me, it's all an exchange, you know. It's an exchange between the student and the teacher, an exchange between the writer and the culture. The culture exists apart from the writer and the writer hopes to bring his or her individuality to bear on the culture, but also to be penetrated by the culture, so that the product is a recognizable cultural product but also unique to that writer. I have to believe simultaneously in the individuality of the writer and the reality of the culture, that they both exist and that there can be an exchange between the two. And to believe that is basically to have a formalist, or structuralist, theory of literature. That's what I have and that's how I do it.

Q: In one way you sound similar to William Stafford in his poetry workshops. He is also nonjudgmental. But at the same time, I've heard he's passive in class. You're not passive.

No, I'm not. Because I also want them to have a theoretical basis: I want them to have *my* theoretical basis. They can have another one later, but I want them to have mine in my class. Lots of times students resist on all kinds of grounds. They don't want to do it my way. What I always say to them is, "Before you drop the class, remember, you will always do it your way. I just want you to do it my way for four months, just to see if you can learn something from my way."

Q: Tell me about the rituals of evasion you mentioned earlier.

They involve being willing to give up rituals that you've already developed as a writer. Let's say a student says to me, "Well, I write one draft and then I put it away for six months and then come back to it." That's a question of evasion of commitment. When I say commitment to the work, I mean the willingness to take up a set of characters or themes or actions that you really want to explore, to fiddle with it and change it and work on it consistently until you feel like you've explored it as well as you can. I think what a lot of students do, and maybe a lot of writers do, too, is develop rituals which don't actually allow them to spend time with or become engaged with their chosen themes or characters.

Sometimes you'll have students who, no matter how much a story demands big changes, will focus on sentences and fiddle with this one and that one obsessively. Or, I had a student whose evasion was never to take one piece to completion. He would write a first draft and take every little criticism as an occasion for totally blowing out the first draft and going on with something completely different. He'd come back with the story that he'd said was the second draft but it was just not recognizably related to the first draft in any way. That was a kind of evasion, too, because his talent was invention. Since he had no control, he had to be made to gain control, whereas a lot of other students who have no real invention have to be made to invent new themes and new characters, instead of fiddling with one or two sentences or touching up an ending.

Q: Doesn't that place a burden on you to see each writer individually: what they're good at, what methods of evasion they use?

But that's the thing about this revision method. I see sixteen drafts over sixteen weeks, so it becomes pretty clear what each student's repeated evasions are.

The other thing is, I never would go back to the normal workshop method, where I read a story once and then talk about it, because I now don't believe I ever really understand what the student is doing in the first draft. I mean, increasingly I feel it takes me to the third or even fourth draft to really get a handle on what's going on in the story, me and the class both, seeing the suggestions we've made that haven't worked out, earlier analyses of the story we've made that have been wrong.

And we haven't even talked about all these issues from the point of view of the class, as opposed to the point of view of the writer. It's a much more interesting class session because the students have a larger investment in each other's writing. They make suggestions; they say "do this, do that," and a week later they see the results. The students are more committed to one another's work over the course of the semester and that builds a sense of *esprit de corps*—or it can; it doesn't necessarily, but it can. And it becomes an ongoing dialogue about a given story. In a good class—and not every class is good—the other students come to have a real attachment to the writer's characters and the writer's themes and the writer's stories.

This leads to what I think is the biggest drawback to my method, and maybe a reason why sixteen weeks is enough. And that is, often by the end of the class we can't read each other's stories anymore, because we do have an investment in them. Usually at the end I say, "Now it's time for you to show these stories to fresh readers." As hard as we try to be critical for sixteen weeks, pretty soon familiarity begins to overwhelm our critical faculties.

Q: William Gass, who you mentioned earlier, said in a Paris Review *interview, "I resent spending a lot of time on lousy stuff. If somebody is reading a bad paper in a seminar, it is nevertheless on Plato, and it is Plato we can talk about. Whereas if somebody is writing about their hunting trip—well—where can one go for salvation or relief?" Does your use of an analytical method, from a personal point of view, ease your burden emotionally as a teacher?*

Oh, sure. It used to be a trial. I don't feel that way anymore, even with undergraduate stories. I think it's because the pleasure of analysis is various enough that if you bring an analytical frame of mind to almost anything you can enjoy it. And I do find that since I am no longer looking at the stories as "good" or "bad," there is a kind of alienation I no longer feel.

I have a friend whose basis of teaching writing is really judgmental, and he can barely stand to read their stories. I don't want to criticize him, but I think it's all part and parcel; they resent him for not liking their stories, even if it's all unspoken, and he resents them for writing bad stories. The key is not thinking of them as "good" and "bad" but thinking of them as examples of some mode of analysis that can be used in an educating way.

Now, we can go back and say—or maybe Gass would say—that some stories are so bad to begin with you're grateful for anything by the time you're into the third draft. And in a less negative way maybe I would say that, too. If I were William Gass, I might say that, having been aware of how far from my intellectual standard students had been, I now recognize how suddenly and in some sense surprisingly they were approaching it.

But all that does is say they're educable, and that writing fiction is a learnable skill. I think there are plenty of people in the world who don't feel that way. In some sense, if they're writers, it's somehow self-aggrandizing to feel that way because then they're saying they never learned anything, they just burst full-blown onto the scene as fully developed writers. Well, that may be true if you've written one or two books and don't know where it came from, but if you've written eight or ten or twelve books and can look back and see the progress in your work, then you know that at some point you were *less* competent and now you are *more* competent.

Q: But the question remains whether people recognize being helped along the way, or whether they feel simply self-taught.

Sure, and maybe they *weren't* helped along the way, maybe they did put it together on their own.

Q: As you seemed to have done.

Well, I think I wasn't, let's say, wonderfully analyzed along the way.

Q: You never had that idealized mentor–protégé relationship, where someone took you under their wing and you suddenly blossomed? That wasn't part of your particular development?

No, but I did blossom, and in a semester—but in some sense I don't know why. It still took me a long time after that to write a publishable story. I also think there's a distinct break in my work between *Duplicate Keys*, which is my third novel, and *The Greenlanders*, which is my fourth. What I always imagined people saying in reviews of *The Greenlanders*, but nobody did, was, "Who would ever expect *this* from the person who wrote *Duplicate Keys*?" I mean, *Duplicate Keys* is a competent murder mystery. It's all about New York, and it's fun. But I underwent a significant aesthetic sea change between those two novels and I don't know why. It had nothing to do with teachers or anything like that.

Q: An added dimensional quality?

Well, I think it was about engaging ideas and emotions that were long-standing. I felt very apocalyptic as a child, because I grew up in the fifties with the atom bomb, and when I went to Iceland in 1977 and discovered that people had lived on Greenland for 450 years or more and then disappeared, that really appealed to a part of me that had been afraid of that precise thing. And there was another part of me that was really taken with the tone that was part of Icelandic literature in particular and Scandinavian literature in general. There's a kind of dryness and recognition of the workings of evil and expectation of the worst in some ways, and a very interesting and subtle understatement and irony, which has always appealed to me. So there were a lot of things that came together when I wrote *The Greenlanders*.

Q: Is there an ordered, inevitable world in that literature? I don't know it very well.

I think so. What happened in Greenland was predicted by Norse myth, which predicts the end of the human world. It's the only mythical system that has an unhappy ending. No one comes to redeem the human world. It's predicted that the gods will finally come to a great battle with the forces of evil, but the gods will fall short; the forces of evil will overwhelm the world. Well, the only happy ending is that all the warriors will get to have one last fling before the final darkness.

I have never heard of another mythical system that predicts the end of the world, and in Greenland it happened, the world ended by the degree to which the people overextended themselves by living there. The history of Greenland is about how much margin you have for survival. And in some sense the early history of Scandinavia is about that, too, but then the modern world came along and expanded their margin just in time.

What I'm saying is, I found something that appealed to me on some kind of deep aesthetic level in Icelandic and Scandinavian literature. I came to know I'm very susceptible to it. So, as I look back on my career, I see that I was educable. When I look at my students, I see that they are educable, too: When, over three drafts, they progress from farther from the ideal to nearer the ideal, that's when I put my judgment of their work in abeyance; I don't feel I have a right to judge.

Even the least competent writer is unique. They are, just by definition, themselves. But they should come up with something that is not only unique but also interesting. The problem is, who's interesting when they're nineteen; who's even interesting when they're twenty-five, the age of most graduate writing students? And so I think any educator who disdains his students because they're not interesting or good is not an educator, not really interested in students; he's interested in other aspects of university life. I see teaching in some sense as a *pro bono* thing. You give back what you received.

Q: It's a pleasure, in that sense?

And the pleasure's enhanced all the time. I had a student who didn't have a great sense of grammar, the stories were very trite, typical undergraduate stories. But he finally decided to work through his revisions of a story, and it was very easy to see as the story progressed that he did bring his own original vision to it. It still wasn't a publishable story, but it was enjoyable to us. Once again, it's a lesson to me that you can't count out any, any, *any* student.

Q: A number of teachers have said that the good students will write well without help anyway.

Well, I would agree, but they might not get as far as quickly. If you can give them the right teaching, maybe you can help them not reinvent the wheel. I don't know what you can give the good ones, but the ones who aren't so good, who don't have native talent, those can get published if they have a great deal of drive and something to say.

And then there's this other whole group who will never get published but who will conform to other kinds of educational goals. They'll get a new appreciation and a new interest in writing and reading. So in some sense you're teaching the writers who will come after you, and in another sense you're teaching your readers. Not every student of philosophy is going to be a philosopher, but if you're a philosophy teacher you hope they'll approach their life with a moment's pause once in a while because you've taught them ethics. Well, if you're a teacher of writing you hope they'll approach their writing life with pause before they go buy another Danielle Steele novel. Maybe, just maybe, they'll buy something else because you taught them something.

SELECTED BIBLIOGRAPHY

The following books have been particularly helpful to me in connection with this project.

Aldridge, John W. *Talents and Technicians: Literary Chic and the New Assembly-Line Fiction*. New York: Scribner's, 1992.

The AWP Official Guide to Writing Programs. Paradise, Calif.: Dustbooks, 1992. [Or contact: The Associated Writing Programs, Old Dominion University, Norfolk, Va. 23529-0079.]

Baumbach, Jonathan, ed. *Writers as Teachers/Teachers as Writers*. New York: Holt, Rinehart & Winston, 1970.

Dillard, R.H.W. *Understanding George Garrett*. Columbia, S.C.: University of South Carolina Press, 1988.

Gardner, John. *On Becoming a Novelist*. New York: Harper & Row, 1983.

–. *The Art of Fiction*. New York: Alfred A. Knopf, 1984.

Hill, Jane. *Gail Godwin*. New York: Twayne Publishers, 1992.

Huddle, David. *The Writing Habit: Essays*. Layton, Utah: Gibbs Smith, 1991.

Hugo, Richard. *The Triggering Town*. New York: W. W. Norton & Co., 1979.

Moxley, Joseph M., ed. *Creative Writing in America: Theory and Pedagogy*. Urbana, Ill.: National Council of Teachers of English, 1989.

O'Connor, Flannery. *Mystery and Manners*. New York: Farrar, Straus & Giroux, 1961.

Pack, Robert, and Jay Parini, eds. *Writers on Writing*. Middlebury, Vt.: Middlebury College Press, 1991.

Pearlman, Mickey, and Katherine Usher Henderson. *A Voice of One's Own: Conversations with America's Writing Women.* New York: Houghton Mifflin, 1990.

Shapiro, Nancy Larson, and Ron Padgett, eds. *The Point: Where Teaching & Writing Intersect.* New York: Teachers and Writers Collaborative, 1983.

Stegner, Wallace. *Wallace Stegner: On the Teaching of Creative Writing.* Edited by Edward Connery Lathem. Hanover, New Hampshire: University Press of New England, 1988.

INDEX

ABOUT THE AUTHOR

Alexander Neubauer is an author of both fiction and nonfiction works, including *Nature's Thumbprint*. He is also a teacher of creative writing at The New School for Social Research in New York. He and his wife, the writer April Stevens, live with their two cats in Manhattan and on a farm in northwestern Connecticut.